INTRODUCING
ISSUES WITH
OPPOSING
VIEWPOINTS®

Smoking

Noël Merino, *Book Editor*

GREENHAVEN PRESS
A part of Gale, Cengage Learning

GALE
CENGAGE Learning™

Detroit • New York • San Francisco • New Haven, Conn • Waterville, Maine • London

GALE
CENGAGE Learning

Christine Nasso, *Publisher*
Elizabeth Des Chenes, *Managing Editor*

For more information, contact:
Greenhaven Press
27500 Drake Rd.
Farmington Hills, MI 48331-3535
Or you can visit our Internet site at gale.cengage.com

For product information and technology assistance, contact us at

Gale Customer Support, 1-800-877-4253
For permission to use material from this text or product, submit all requests online at www.cengage.com/permissions

Further permissions questions can be e-mailed to permissionrequest@cengage.com

Articles in Greenhaven Press anthologies are often edited for length to meet page requirements. In addition, original titles of these works are changed to clearly present the main thesis and to explicitly indicate the author's opinion. Every effort is made to ensure that Greenhaven Press accurately reflects the original intent of the authors. Every effort has been made to trace the owners of copyrighted material.

Cover image © Jaubert Images/Alamy.

LIBRARY OF CONGRESS CATALOGING-IN-PUBLICATION DATA

Smoking / Noël Merino, book editor.
    p. cm. -- (Introducing issues with opposing viewpoints)
 Includes bibliographical references and index.
 ISBN 978-0-7377-5101-7 (hbk.)
 1. Smoking--Juvenile literature. I. Merino, Noël.
 HV5740.S6185 2010
 362.29'6--dc22
 	
                                                                    2010026766

Printed in the United States of America
1 2 3 4 5 6 7 14 13 12 11 10

Contents

Foreword

Indulging in a wide spectrum of ideas, beliefs, and perspectives is a critical cornerstone of democracy. After all, it is often debates over differences of opinion, such as whether to legalize abortion, how to treat prisoners, or when to enact the death penalty, that shape our society and drive it forward. Such diversity of thought is frequently regarded as the hallmark of a healthy and civilized culture. As the Reverend Clifford Schutjer of the First Congregational Church in Mansfield, Ohio, declared in a 2001 sermon, "Surrounding oneself with only like-minded people, restricting what we listen to or read only to what we find agreeable is irresponsible. Refusing to entertain doubts once we make up our minds is a subtle but deadly form of arrogance." With this advice in mind, Introducing Issues with Opposing Viewpoints books aim to open readers' minds to the critically divergent views that comprise our world's most important debates.

Introducing Issues with Opposing Viewpoints simplifies for students the enormous and often overwhelming mass of material now available via print and electronic media. Collected in every volume is an array of opinions that captures the essence of a particular controversy or topic. Introducing Issues with Opposing Viewpoints books embody the spirit of nineteenth-century journalist Charles A. Dana's axiom: "Fight for your opinions, but do not believe that they contain the whole truth, or the only truth." Absorbing such contrasting opinions teaches students to analyze the strength of an argument and compare it to its opposition. From this process readers can inform and strengthen their own opinions, or be exposed to new information that will change their minds. Introducing Issues with Opposing Viewpoints is a mosaic of different voices. The authors are statesmen, pundits, academics, journalists, corporations, and ordinary people who have felt compelled to share their experiences and ideas in a public forum. Their words have been collected from newspapers, journals, books, speeches, interviews, and the Internet, the fastest growing body of opinionated material in the world.

Introducing Issues with Opposing Viewpoints shares many of the well-known features of its critically acclaimed parent series, Opposing Viewpoints. The articles are presented in a pro/con format, allowing readers to absorb divergent perspectives side by side. Active reading questions preface each viewpoint, requiring the student to approach the material thoughtfully and carefully. Useful charts, graphs, and cartoons supplement each article. A thorough introduction provides readers with crucial background on an issue. An annotated bibliography points the reader toward articles, books, and Web sites that contain additional information on the topic. An appendix of organizations to contact contains a wide variety of charities, nonprofit organizations, political groups, and private enterprises that each hold a position on the issue at hand. Finally, a comprehensive index allows readers to locate content quickly and efficiently.

Introducing Issues with Opposing Viewpoints is also significantly different from Opposing Viewpoints. As the series title implies, its presentation will help introduce students to the concept of opposing viewpoints, and learn to use this material to aid in critical writing and debate. The series' four-color, accessible format makes the books attractive and inviting to readers of all levels. In addition, each viewpoint has been carefully edited to maximize a reader's understanding of the content. Short but thorough viewpoints capture the essence of an argument. A substantial, thought-provoking essay question placed at the end of each viewpoint asks the student to further investigate the issues raised in the viewpoint, compare and contrast two authors' arguments, or consider how one might go about forming an opinion on the topic at hand. Each viewpoint contains sidebars that include at-a-glance information and handy statistics. A Facts About section located in the back of the book further supplies students with relevant facts and figures.

Following in the tradition of the Opposing Viewpoints series, Greenhaven Press continues to provide readers with invaluable exposure to the controversial issues that shape our world. As John Stuart Mill once wrote: "The only way in which a human being can make some approach to knowing the whole of a subject is by hearing what can be said about it by persons of every variety of opinion and studying all modes in which it can be looked at by every character of mind. No wise man ever acquired his wisdom in any mode but this." It is to this principle that Introducing Issues with Opposing Viewpoints books are dedicated.

Introduction

"Third-hand smoke is tobacco smoke contamination that remains after the cigarette has been extinguished."[1]
—Jonathan Winickoff, Department of Pediatrics,
Harvard Medical School

The social acceptance of smoking in public places has diminished rapidly in the last few decades, largely due to concerns about harms to nonsmokers. Prior to 1990 smoking in workplaces, in restaurants, and on planes was the norm. Since the 1990s, smoking bans have gradually become the norm in public places. The main justification for such bans has been concern about the health risks of secondhand smoke. More recently, concern has been raised about the health risks of so-called thirdhand smoke.

Secondhand smoke is the smoke from a burning cigarette, cigar, or pipe, or the smoke exhaled by a person who is smoking. According to the National Cancer Institute, a part of the U.S. National Institutes of Health, "Of the more than 4,000 chemicals that have been identified in secondhand tobacco smoke, at least 250 are known to be harmful, and 50 of these are known to cause cancer."[2] The National Cancer Institute claims that approximately 3,000 lung cancer deaths occur each year among nonsmokers because of exposure to secondhand smoke. The National Cancer Institute also claims that secondhand smoke is the cause of a variety of other harmful health effects, including 46,000 heart disease deaths each year. It is largely because of the belief that secondhand smoke causes health effects in nonsmokers that smoking has been banned from public places such as workplaces, planes, and restaurants.

Recently, concerns have been raised about the harmful effects of smoke after a smoker has extinguished a cigarette, cigar, or pipe. In a 2009 interview pediatrician Jonathan P. Winickoff of the Harvard Medical School defines thirdhand smoke as "tobacco smoke contamination that remains after the cigarette has been extinguished." He argues, "Third-hand smoke refers to the tobacco toxins that build up over time—one cigarette will coat the surface of a certain room." Winickoff also claims, "Smokers themselves are also contaminated . . .

smokers actually emit toxins." He claims that the risks of this third-hand smoke, or residual toxins, are particularly harmful for infants and children because of their greater susceptibility to toxins. Winick-off hopes that increased knowledge about the dangers of thirdhand smoke will encourage parents to never smoke inside their homes, even when children are not present; and he hopes that ultimately smokers will quit: "That's the only way to completely protect their children."[3]

In an article published in 2009, Winickoff and other scholars claim, "Research has documented the association between smoking in the home and persistently high levels of tobacco toxins well beyond the period of active smoking."[4] Winickoff and his colleagues performed a study where they surveyed people and asked whether they agreed with the following statement: "Breathing air in a room today where people smoked yesterday can harm the health of infants and children." What they found in their survey was "an independent association be-tween the health belief that thirdhand smoke harms children and strict no-smoking policies in the home," concluding that "emphasizing that thirdhand smoke harms the health of children may be an important element in encouraging home smoking bans."[5]

Not everyone is convinced that the science supports the dangers of so-called thirdhand smoke. Michael Siegel, a professor of public health at Boston University, responded to Winickoff and his colleagues by stating, "I am not convinced that the existing scientific evidence sup-ports the conclusion that thirdhand smoke poses a significant public health hazard, even to children living in homes with a smoker." Siegel questions the claim that smokers need to worry about thirdhand smoke residue left on clothing, calling it "merely a theoretical concern." Siegel worries that focusing on what he believes is an unsupported concern about thirdhand smoke may "backfire by undermining people's ap-preciation of the documented hazards of secondhand smoke."[6] Siegel believes that the scientific evidence does support the risks of second-hand smoke and that public policy should focus on encouraging par-ents not to smoke around children rather than possibly giving them the idea that if they have smoke on their clothes they may as well smoke around their kids if they are not going to quit.

Some critics are worried that discussion of thirdhand smoke is part of a larger trend to advance the anti-smoking movement no matter what the science supports. Author Christopher Snowdon echoes Siegel's concern about the study cited by Winickoff regarding thirdhand smoke: "Since the end justifies the means in the world of tobacco control, thirdhand smoke is useful if it helps to modify the public's behaviour and of little interest if it doesn't. Whether the theory is actually valid or not is of secondary importance. Like a religion, thirdhand smoke is about faith, not science, for there is no science to mention."[7]

In February 2010, a study in *Proceeding of the National Academy of Sciences of the United States of America* also raised concern about thirdhand smoke, concluding that residual nicotine left behind by secondhand smoke could pose health hazards. Siegel and others also criticized this study. The debate about thirdhand smoke is likely to continue and could raise an interesting issue. If smokers themselves are toxic, as the two studies suggest, will smokers themselves be banned from public places? This is just one of the fascinating controversies raised by the issue of smoking. Many other issues, including the debate about the harms of firsthand and secondhand smoke, the debate about legal restrictions on smoking, and an exploration of competing suggestions for social policies addressing smoking are explored in *Introducing Issues with Opposing Viewpoints: Smoking.*

Notes

1. National Cancer Institute, "Secondhand Smoke: Questions and Answers," revised August 1, 2007. www.cancer.gov/cancertopics/factsheet/Tobacco/ETS/print?page=&keyword=.
2. Jonathan P. Winickoff, quoted in Coco Ballantyne, "What Is Third-Hand Smoke? Is It Dangerous?" *Scientific American*, January 6, 2009. www.scientificamerican.com/article.cfm?id=what-is-third-hand-smoke.
3. Winickoff, in Ballantyne, "What Is Third-Hand Smoke?"
4. Jonathan P. Winickoff, et al., "Beliefs About the Health Effects of 'Thirdhand' Smoke and Home Smoking Bans," *Pediatrics*, vol. 123, no. 1, January 2009, pp. e74–75.
5. Winickoff, et al., "Beliefs About the Health Effects of 'Thirdhand' Smoke and Home Smoking Bans," p. e78.
6. Michael Siegel, "New Study Warns of Dangers of 'Thirdhand' Tobacco Smoke," The Rest of the Story: Tobacco News Analysis and

Commentary, January 5, 2009. http://tobaccoanalysis.blogspot
.com/2009/01/new-study-warns-of-dangers-of-thirdhand.html.

7. Christopher Snowdon, "Beyond Belief," VelvetGloveIronFist.com,
January 8, 2009. http://velvetgloveironfist.com/thirdhandsmoke
.php.

Chapter 1

Is Smoking a Serious Problem?

The debate about smoking being a serious problem is happening continuously throughout the United States and abroad.

Tobacco Use, Including Smoking, Leads to Serious Health Risks

"Tobacco use is the leading preventable cause of disease, disability, and death in the United States."

National Institute on Drug Abuse

In the following viewpoint the National Institute on Drug Abuse (NIDA) argues that tobacco use, including smoking cigarettes, has several negative health effects. NIDA contends that the nicotine in tobacco has harmful effects on the brain, causing dangerous long-term changes. Smoking cigarettes, NIDA argues, is a particularly harmful method of using tobacco, accounting for the development of many diseases, including cancer. Finally, since tobacco use leads to addiction, quitting often requires several attempts and treatment of the addiction. NIDA is part of the National Institutes of Health, a component of the U.S. Department of Health and Human Services.

Cigarettes and Other Tobacco Products, National Institute on Drug Abuse, National Institute of Health, U.S. Department of Health and Human Services, June 2009.

AS YOU READ, CONSIDER THE FOLLOWING QUESTIONS:

1. According to the author, what is the addictive drug contained within cigarettes and other forms of tobacco?
2. Cigarette smoking, according to the National Institute on Drug Abuse, accounts for what fraction of all cancers?
3. The author contends that rates of relapse for smoking cessation diminish considerably after how long?

Tobacco use is the leading preventable cause of disease, disability, and death in the United States. Between 1964 and 2004, cigarette smoking caused an estimated 12 million deaths, including 4.1 million deaths from cancer, 5.5 million deaths from cardiovascular diseases, 1.1 million deaths from respiratory diseases, and 94,000 infant deaths related to mothers smoking during pregnancy. According to the Centers for Disease Control and Prevention (CDC), cigarette smoking results in more than 400,000 premature deaths in the United States each year—about 1 in every 5 U.S. deaths.

Tobacco's Effect on the Brain

Cigarettes and other forms of tobacco—including cigars, pipe tobacco, snuff, and chewing tobacco—contain the addictive drug nicotine. Nicotine is readily absorbed into the bloodstream when a tobacco product is chewed, inhaled, or smoked. A typical smoker will take 10 puffs on a cigarette over a period of 5 minutes that the cigarette is lit. Thus, a person who smokes about 1 1/2 packs (30 cigarettes) daily gets 300 "hits" of nicotine each day.

Upon entering the bloodstream, nicotine immediately stimulates the adrenal glands to release the hormone epinephrine (adrenaline). Epinephrine stimulates the central nervous system and increases blood pressure, respiration, and heart rate. Glucose is released into the blood while nicotine suppresses insulin output from the pancreas, which means that smokers have chronically elevated blood sugar levels.

Like cocaine, heroin, and marijuana, nicotine increases levels of the neurotransmitter dopamine, which affects the brain pathways that control reward and pleasure. For many tobacco users, long-term brain

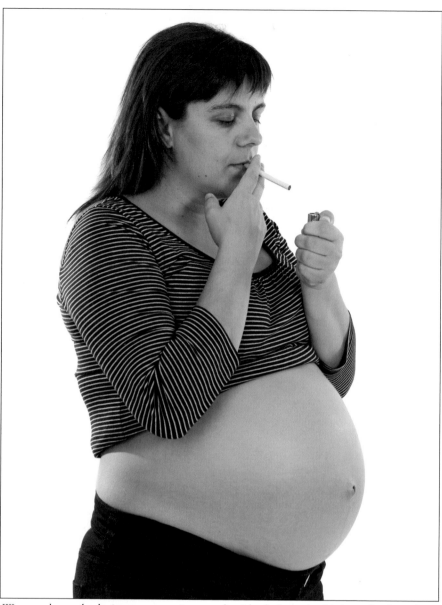

Women who smoke during pregnancy increase the risk of adverse health issues for themselves and for their unborn children.

changes induced by continued nicotine exposure result in addiction—a condition of compulsive drug seeking and use, even in the face of negative consequences. Studies suggest that additional compounds in tobacco smoke, such as acetaldehyde, may enhance nicotine's effects on the brain. A number of studies indicate that adolescents are especially vulnerable to these effects and may be more likely than adults to develop an addiction to tobacco.

When an addicted user tries to quit, he or she experiences withdrawal symptoms including powerful cravings for tobacco, irritability, difficulty paying attention, sleep disturbances, and increased appetite. Treatments can help smokers manage these symptoms and improve the likelihood of successfully quitting.

Adverse Health Effects of Tobacco

Cigarette smoking accounts for about one-third of all cancers, including 90 percent of lung cancer cases. In addition to cancer, smoking causes lung diseases such as chronic bronchitis and emphysema, and increases the risk of heart disease, including stroke, heart attack, vascular disease, and aneurysm. Smoking has also been linked to leukemia, cataracts, and pneumonia. On average, adults who smoke die 14 years earlier than nonsmokers.

Although nicotine is addictive and can be toxic if ingested in high doses, it does not cause cancer—other chemicals are responsible for most of the severe health consequences of tobacco use. Tobacco smoke is a complex mixture of chemicals such as carbon monoxide, tar, formaldehyde, cyanide, and ammonia—many of which are known carcinogens. Carbon monoxide increases the chance of cardiovascular diseases. Tar exposes the user to an increased risk of lung cancer, emphysema, and bronchial disorders. Smokeless tobacco (such as chewing tobacco and snuff) also increases the risk of cancer, especially oral cancers.

Pregnant women who smoke cigarettes run an increased risk of miscarriage, stillborn or premature infants, or infants with low birthweight. Maternal smoking may

FAST FACT

The relationship between smoking and lung cancer was first classified as causal in a 1964 report of the U.S. Surgeon General.

also be associated with learning and behavioral problems in children. Smoking more than one pack of cigarettes per day during pregnancy nearly doubles the risk that the affected child will become addicted to tobacco if that child starts smoking.

While we often think of medical consequences that result from direct use of tobacco products, passive or secondary smoke also increases the risk for many diseases. Secondhand smoke, also known as environmental tobacco smoke, consists of exhaled smoke and smoke given off by the burning end of tobacco products. According to CDC, approximately 38,000 deaths per year can be attributed to secondhand smoke. Nonsmokers exposed to secondhand smoke at home or work increase their risk of developing heart disease by 25 to 30 percent and lung cancer by 20 to 30 percent. In addition, secondhand smoke causes respiratory problems in nonsmokers, such as coughing, phlegm, and reduced lung function. Children exposed to secondhand smoke are at an increased risk for sudden infant death syndrome, acute respiratory infections, ear problems, and more severe asthma.

Although quitting can be difficult, the health benefits of smoking cessation are immediate and substantial—including reduced risk for cancers, heart disease, and stroke. A 35-year-old man who quits smoking will, on average, increase his life expectancy by 5 years.

Dealing with Tobacco Addiction

Tobacco addiction is a chronic disease that often requires multiple attempts to quit. Although some smokers are able to quit without help, many others need assistance. Generally, rates of relapse for smoking cessation are highest in the first few weeks and months and diminish considerably after about 3 months. Both behavioral interventions (counseling) and medication can help smokers quit; the combination of medication with counseling is more effective than either alone.

Behavioral treatments employ a variety of methods to assist smokers in quitting, ranging from self-help materials to individual counseling. These interventions teach individuals to recognize high-risk situations and develop coping strategies to deal with them. The U.S. Department of Health and Human Services' (HHS) national toll-free quitline, 800-QUIT-NOW, is an access point for any smoker seeking information and assistance in quitting.

Nicotine replacement therapies (NRTs), such as nicotine gum and the nicotine patch, were the first pharmacological treatments approved by the Food and Drug Administration (FDA) for use in smoking cessation therapy. NRTs deliver a controlled dose of nicotine to a smoker in order to relieve withdrawal symptoms during the smoking cessa-

Deaths Attributable to Individual Risk (in 1,000s)

Risk	Number of Deaths
Smoking	467
High blood pressure	395
Overweight-obesity (high BMI)	216
Physical inactivity	191
High blood glucose	190
High LDL cholesterol	113
High dietary sodium (salt)	102

Taken from: Goodarz Danaei, Eric L. Ding, Dariush Mozaffarian, et al., "The Preventable Causes of Death in the United States: Comparative Risk Assessment of Dietary, Lifestyle, and Metabolic Risk Factors," *PLoS Medicine*, April 2009.

tion process. They are most successful when used in combination with behavioral treatments. FDA-approved NRT products include nicotine chewing gum, the nicotine transdermal patch, nasal sprays, inhalers, and lozenges.

Bupropion and varenicline are two FDA-approved non-nicotine medications that effectively increase rates of long-term abstinence from smoking. Bupropion, a medication that goes by the trade name Zyban, was approved by the FDA in 1997 for use in smoking cessation. Varenicline tartrate (trade name: Chantix) targets nicotine receptors in the brain, easing withdrawal symptoms and blocking the effects of nicotine if people resume smoking.

Scientists are currently pursuing many other avenues of research to develop new tobacco cessation therapies. One promising intervention is a vaccine that targets nicotine, blocking the drug's access to the brain and preventing its reinforcing effects. Preliminary trials of this vaccine have yielded promising results.

EVALUATING THE AUTHORS' ARGUMENTS:

In this viewpoint the National Institute on Drug Abuse (NIDA) contends that tobacco use, including smoking, poses serious risks to health. What is the key point of disagreement between NIDA and Philip Alcabes, author of the next viewpoint?

Smoking, Not Tobacco Use, Leads to Serious Health Risks

Philip Alcabes

"Tobacco is not deadly; the harm is in the smoke."

In the following viewpoint Philip Alcabes argues that the campaign against tobacco use is misguided. Alcabes claims that it is smoke, not nicotine, that leads to health risks. He contends that there are nicotine delivery alternatives that are much safer than smoking and laments the fact that these alternatives are not being pursued. Philip Alcabes is professor of urban public health at Hunter College's School of Health Sciences of the City University of New York. He is the author of *Dread: How Fear and Fantasy Have Fueled Epidemics from the Black Death to Avian Flu*.

Philip Alcabes, "Blowing Smoke About Tobacco," *Washington Post*, May 30, 2006. Reproduced by permission of the author.

"Tobacco: deadly in any form or disguise" is the slogan of the World Health Organization's World No Tobacco Day tomorrow [May 31, 2006]. The claim is false: Tobacco is not deadly; the harm is in the smoke. A policy that confuses innocuous tobacco with harmful smoke is responsible for millions of avoidable deaths each year worldwide.

The Nicotine Abstinence Policy

Cigarette smoke is a deadly delivery device for a benign but habit-forming product: nicotine. Nicotine isn't especially dangerous—about like caffeine. Good policy toward tobacco use would reduce the grave harm of smoking by replacing cigarettes with non-smoked forms of nicotine for the addicts. They might use nicotine safely forever, if harmless delivery systems were widely available.

Instead, nicotine abstinence is the policymakers' only approach to tobacco. Like other abstinence campaigns (alcohol prohibition, sexual abstinence before marriage, just saying "no" to drugs), this one is both moralistic and ineffective.

The human cost of the nicotine-abstinence policy is doleful. More than 430,000 U.S. deaths each year—one out of every five—can be attributed to smoking. This is 10 times our death rate from car crashes, 30 times the rate from AIDS—an unprecedented toll that is a testament to the inadequacy of 40 years of quit-smoking policy.

The surgeon general reported smoking to be a health hazard back in 1964, but the net effect of smoking-cessation messages since then is that between 4 and 5 percent of smokers quit each year. Of the approximately 14 million Americans who try to quit smoking every year, only 2 million succeed. That failure leaves 45 million to 60 million American smokers, more than one-fifth of American adults. Most of them smoke regularly. Another million or so start smoking each year. In fact, of all the Americans alive today who ever smoked regularly, half are smoking now.

A Smokeless Alternative

Obviously, nicotine use is a popular and tenacious habit. Equally obviously, tobacco policy is a failure. Surveys show that a majority of current smokers would like good alternatives to smoking as ways of getting nicotine. But we will not tell nicotine users that there are safe ways to continue to use the legal drug they crave. Apparently, our policymakers would rather see those people get sick and die.

Alternative nicotine delivery could be easy. Nicotine replacement therapy could work long-term. Gum and the patch are already available, but not to everyone. Also, they are still approved only for short-term use and can deliver only small doses—inadequate for heavy users.

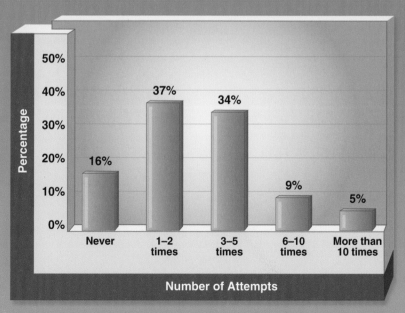

Taken from: "Smoking Habits Stable; Most Would Like to Quit," Gallup, July 18, 2006.
[http://www.gallup.com/poll/23791/Smoking-Habits-Stable-Most-Would-Like-Quit.aspx].

A student of the Federal University of Rio de Janeiro passes out handouts describing the dangers of smoking in celebration of the World No Tobacco Day. This author feels that the smoke is the health hazard, not the tobacco.

Smokeless tobacco would work. It comes in several forms. One is chewing tobacco, made famous by cowboys and ballplayers. But other forms are handier, less messy and far less dangerous than smoking. Yet health officials label smokeless tobacco as "not a safe alternative to smoking," despite much evidence that it is quite safe. Indeed, current policy is so wedded to nicotine abstinence that officials will lie to discourage widespread use of smokeless tobacco as a way of delivering the drug.

As Carl V. Phillips, an epidemiologist at the University of Alberta, has shown, evidence points to a low risk of health hazards stemming from smokeless-tobacco use. That includes virtually no evidence of risk of oral cancer. Phillips's calculations show that total mortality from "smokeless" is about a hundredth of that from smoking.

A Deadly Crusade

And then there's what many smokers nowadays really do: Mix periods of abstinence (encouraged by smoke-free workplaces and restaurants) with periods of light smoking. Mixing light or occasional smoking with other nicotine-delivery products might be even safer—but it can't be studied as a possible alternative because current funding goes only to research on how to quit smoking, not on finding a safe level of smoking.

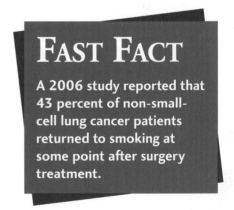

FAST FACT

A 2006 study reported that 43 percent of non-small-cell lung cancer patients returned to smoking at some point after surgery treatment.

How shameful that the United States is willing to allow almost a half-million Americans to die each year, and that the World Health Organization is prepared to allow up to 5 million annual deaths worldwide—all because of a delivery device—cigarette smoke—whose hazards are well known and largely avoidable.

Where's the usually progressive public-health establishment on this? We are generally not given to telling people, "Stop doing what you are doing." We prefer health promotion in the form of seat belts, motorcycle helmets, condoms, syringe exchange, ingredient labels, and warning labels, rather than forcing people to quit their habits. But with tobacco we have jettisoned our tolerance and thrown all our support to nicotine abstinence.

We cannot ignore tobacco in its one deadly "disguise": cigarette smoke. Neither should we ignore a deadly nicotine-abstinence crusade disguised as tobacco control.

EVALUATING THE AUTHORS' ARGUMENTS:

In this viewpoint Alcabes claims that nicotine is not especially dangerous. In what way does the National Institute on Drug Abuse, author of the previous viewpoint, specifically dispute this?

Secondhand Smoke Poses Serious Health Risks

National Cancer Institute

"Secondhand smoke causes disease and premature death in nonsmoking adults and children."

In the following viewpoint the U.S. National Cancer Institute (NCI) contends that secondhand smoke causes adverse health effects in nonsmokers. NCI claims that secondhand smoke contains dozens of harmful chemicals, and it causes cancer and other diseases. As a result of the harmful effects of secondhand smoke, NCI claims that no exposure level is safe, and as such, smoking restrictions are becoming more common. NCI is one of twenty-seven institutes and centers that comprise the U.S. National Institutes of Health, which is part of the U.S. Department of Health and Human Services.

Fact Sheet: Secondhand Smoke: Questions and Answers, National Cancer Institute, August 1, 2007.

AS YOU READ, CONSIDER THE FOLLOWING QUESTIONS:
1. According to the author, how many chemicals known to cause cancer are in secondhand smoke?
2. The National Cancer Institute claims that how many lung cancer deaths occur each year from exposure to secondhand smoke?
3. According to the author, what is the only way to fully protect non-smokers from secondhand smoke exposure?

Secondhand smoke (also called environmental tobacco smoke) is the combination of sidestream smoke (the smoke given off by the burning end of a tobacco product) and mainstream smoke (the smoke exhaled by the smoker). Exposure to secondhand smoke is also called involuntary smoking or passive smoking. People are exposed to secondhand smoke in homes, cars, the workplace, and public places such as bars, restaurants, and other recreation settings. In the United States, the source of most secondhand smoke is from cigarettes, followed by pipes, cigars, and other tobacco products.

Chemicals in Secondhand Smoke

Secondhand smoke is measured by testing indoor air for nicotine or other smoke constituents. Exposure to secondhand smoke can be tested by measuring the levels of nicotine (a nicotine by-product in the body) in the nonsmoker's blood, saliva, or urine. Nicotine, cotinine, carbon monoxide, and other evidence of secondhand smoke exposure have been found in the body fluids of nonsmokers exposed to secondhand smoke. . . .

Of the more than 4,000 chemicals that have been identified in secondhand tobacco smoke, at least 250 are known to be harmful, and 50 of these are known to cause cancer. These chemicals include:

- arsenic (a heavy metal toxin)
- benzene (a chemical found in gasoline)
- beryllium (a toxic metal)
- cadmium (a metal used in batteries)
- chromium (a metallic element)

- ethylene oxide (a chemical used to sterilize medical devices)
- nickel (a metallic element)
- polonium-210 (a chemical element that gives off radiation)
- vinyl chloride (a toxic substance used in plastics manufacture)

Many factors affect which chemicals are found in secondhand smoke, including the type of tobacco, the chemicals added to the tobacco, the way the product is smoked, and the paper in which the tobacco is wrapped. . . .

Harmful Effects of Secondhand Smoke

The U.S. Environmental Protection Agency (EPA), the U.S. National Toxicology Program (NTP), the U.S. Surgeon General, and the International Agency for Research on Cancer (IARC) have classified secondhand smoke as a known human carcinogen (cancer-causing agent).

Inhaling secondhand smoke causes lung cancer in nonsmoking adults. Approximately 3,000 lung cancer deaths occur each year among adult nonsmokers in the United States as a result of exposure to secondhand smoke. The Surgeon General estimates that living with a smoker increases a nonsmoker's chances of developing lung cancer by 20 to 30 percent.

Some research suggests that secondhand smoke may increase the risk of breast cancer, nasal sinus cavity cancer, and nasopharyngeal cancer in adults, and leukemia, lymphoma, and brain tumors in children. Additional research is needed to learn whether a link exists between secondhand smoke exposure and these cancers.

FAST FACT

The Institute of Medicine reported in 2009 that evidence supports an association between secondhand-smoke exposure and heart attacks.

Secondhand smoke causes disease and premature death in nonsmoking adults and children. Exposure to secondhand smoke irritates the airways and has immediate harmful effects on a person's heart and blood vessels. It may increase the risk of heart disease by an estimated 25 to 30 percent. In the United States, secondhand smoke is thought to cause about 46,000 heart disease deaths each year. There

Vincent Rennich has worked in casinos for 25 years. He also led the fight to ban smoking in Atlantic City's casinos. Rennich is suing his former employer, Tropicana Casino and Resort, for his lung cancer that he attributes to secondhand smoke in casinos.

may also be a link between exposure to secondhand smoke and the risk of stroke and hardening of the arteries; however, additional research is needed to confirm this link.

Children exposed to secondhand smoke are at an increased risk of sudden infant death syndrome (SIDS), ear infections, colds, pneumonia,

Occupational Exposures to Nicotine Among Groups of Nonsmoking Office Workers

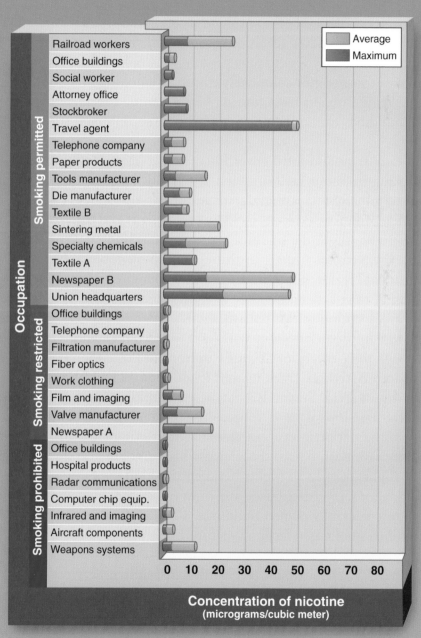

Taken from: U.S. Department of Health & Human Services, "The Health Consequences of Involuntary Exposure to Tobacco Smoke: A Report of the Surgeon General," 2006.

bronchitis, and more severe asthma. Being exposed to secondhand smoke slows the growth of children's lungs and can cause them to cough, wheeze, and feel breathless.

Protecting Nonsmokers from Secondhand Smoke

There is no safe level of exposure to secondhand smoke. Studies have shown that even low levels of secondhand smoke exposure can be harmful. The only way to fully protect nonsmokers from secondhand smoke exposure is to completely eliminate smoking in indoor spaces. Separating smokers from nonsmokers, cleaning the air, and ventilating buildings cannot completely eliminate secondhand smoke exposure.

Many state and local governments have passed laws prohibiting smoking in public facilities such as schools, hospitals, airports, and bus terminals. Increasingly, state and local governments are also requiring private workplaces, including restaurants and bars, to be smoke free. To highlight the significant risk from secondhand smoke exposure, the National Cancer Institute, a component of the National Institutes of Health, holds meetings and conferences in states, counties, cities, or towns that are smoke free, unless certain circumstances justify an exception to this policy.

More information about state-level tobacco regulations is available through the Centers for Disease Control and Prevention (CDC) State Tobacco Activities Tracking and Evaluation (STATE) System Web site. The STATE System is a database containing up-to-date and historical state-level data on tobacco use prevention and control. . . .

On the national level, several laws restricting smoking in public places have been passed. Federal law bans smoking on domestic airline flights, nearly all flights between the United States and foreign destinations, interstate buses, and most trains. Smoking is also banned in most Federally owned buildings. The Pro-Children Act of 1994 prohibits smoking in facilities that routinely provide Federally funded services to children.

The U.S. Department of Health and Human Services (DHHS) *Healthy People 2010*, a comprehensive, nationwide health promotion and disease prevention agenda, includes the goal of reducing the proportion of nonsmokers exposed to secondhand smoke from 65 percent to 45 percent by 2010. . . .

Internationally, several nations, including France, Ireland, New Zealand, Norway, and Uruguay, require all workplaces, including bars and restaurants, to be smoke free.

EVALUATING THE AUTHORS' ARGUMENTS:

In this viewpoint the National Cancer Institute contends that there is no safe level of exposure to secondhand smoke. Does Thomas A. Lambert, author of the following viewpoint, agree or disagree with this? Explain your answer.

The Dangers of Secondhand Smoke Have Been Overstated

Thomas A. Lambert

"One would have to breathe smoke-filled air for 4,000 hours in order to inhale as much tobacco smoke as a smoker inhales in a single cigarette."

In the following viewpoint Thomas A. Lambert argues that the risks of environmental tobacco smoke—that is, secondhand smoke—are not significant enough to warrant some of the restrictions on smoking. Lambert disputes the findings of several agencies regarding secondhand smoke, including the Environmental Protection Agency and the U.S. Surgeon General. Unlike the claims made by many federal agencies, Lambert claims that the evidence shows that environmental tobacco smoke poses only a very minor risk for serious disease. Lambert is associate professor of law at the University of Missouri–Columbia School of Law.

AS YOU READ, CONSIDER THE FOLLOWING QUESTIONS:
1. The author criticizes a study authored by the Environmental Protection Agency that claims how many lung cancer deaths are caused by environmental tobacco smoke, or secondhand smoke?
2. According to Lambert, a 1975 study showed that an hour's worth of exposure to secondhand smoke was equivalent to smoking how many cigarettes?
3. The author supports his viewpoint by referring to a study that collected health data for how many years on thousands of never-smokers who were married to smokers?

I f one were to rely on the stated conclusions of federal agencies (and/or the media reports discussing those conclusions), one might conclude that the risks associated with ETS [environmental tobacco smoke, or secondhand smoke] inhalation do justify significant liberty restrictions. First consider the Environmental Protection Agency's [EPA] 1992 report, *Respiratory Health Effects of Passive Smoking: Lung Cancer and Other Disorders.* That study, which concluded that ETS is a Class A (known human) carcinogen, purported to show that inhalation of ETS causes 3,000 lung cancer deaths per year. Not surprisingly, the study fueled efforts to impose smoking bans.

A Flawed Study

As it turns out, the study hardly amounted to sound science. A congressional inquiry into the methods the EPA used in the study found that "the process at every turn [was] characterized by both scientific and procedural irregularities," including "conflicts of interest by both Agency staff involved in the preparation of the risk assessment and members of the Science Advisory Board panel selected to provide a supposedly independent evaluation of the document." The congressional inquiry further concluded that "the Agency ha[d] deliberately abused and manipulated the scientific data in order to reach a predetermined, politically motivated result."

The findings of the EPA's 1992 study have also been undermined by court opinion. Charged with evaluating the agency's risk assessment

NATIONAL PRESS CLUB

The Health Consequences of Smoking

Then U.S. Surgeon General Richard Carmona released a report on the Health Consequences of Smoking in May 2004. The author of this viewpoint disputes the findings of the Surgeon General's report.

in determining that ETS constitutes a Class A carcinogen, a federal district judge in the case *Flue-Cured Tobacco Coop. Stabilization Corp. v. U.S. EPA* [M.D.N.C. 1994] criticized the agency's analysis in terms that can best be described as scathing. The court concluded:

> [The EPA] publicly committed to a conclusion before research had begun; . . . adjusted established procedure and scientific norms to validate the Agency's public conclusion[;] . . . disregarded infor-

mation and made findings on selective information; did not disseminate significant epidemiologic information; deviated from its Risk Assessment Guidelines; failed to disclose important findings and reasoning; and left significant questions without answers.

Thus, the EPA's purported finding that ETS poses a serious cancer risk—a "finding" that has been extremely influential in motivating state and local smoking bans throughout the United States, should be discounted.

The Surgeon General's Report

Apparently undeterred by these congressional and judicial reprimands, the U.S. surgeon general recently released a report entitled *The Health Consequences of Involuntary Exposure to Tobacco Smoke*, which purports to settle once and for all the debate over the risks of ETS inhalation. In releasing the report, Surgeon General Richard Carmona confidently proclaimed:

> The scientific evidence is now indisputable: secondhand smoke is not a mere annoyance. It is a serious health hazard that can lead to disease and premature death in children and nonsmoking adults.

In presenting the report, the surgeon general's office emphasized to the news media that even brief exposure to ETS poses immediate and significant health risks. The press release accompanying the report stated that "there is no risk-free level of exposure to secondhand smoke" and that "even brief exposure to secondhand smoke has immediate adverse effects on the cardiovascular system and increases risk for heart disease and lung cancer." In his remarks to the media, the surgeon general stated, "Breathing secondhand smoke for even a short time can damage cells and set the cancer process in motion." In a "fact sheet" accompanying the report, the surgeon general explained, "Breathing secondhand smoke for even a short time can have immediate adverse effects on the cardiovascular system." These and similar statements, faithfully repeated by the news media, create the impression that science has determined that simply being in a smoke-filled room exposes one to significant health risks.

Examined closely, the surgeon general's report established no such proposition. The underlying studies upon which the surgeon general's report was based considered the effects of chronic exposure to ETS on individuals, such as long-time spouses of smokers. The studies simply did not consider the health effects of sporadic exposure to ETS and thus cannot provide empirical support for the surgeon general's statements about short-term ETS exposure.

Moreover, those statements are theoretically unsound, for they conflict with the basic toxicological principle that "the dose makes the poison." According to a study published in the *New England Journal of Medicine* in 1975, when many more individuals smoked and there were much higher ETS concentrations in public places, exposure to an hour's worth of prevailing levels of ETS was equivalent to smoking 0.004 cigarettes. Put differently, one would have to breathe smoke-filled air for 4,000 hours in order to inhale as much tobacco smoke as a smoker inhales in a single cigarette. Given those concentration levels, it seems implausible that short-term exposure to ETS poses serious health risks. Possessing neither empirical foundation nor theoretical plausibility, the Surgeon General's public statements about the health risks of brief exposure to ETS were misleading.

But what about the actual findings of the surgeon general's report, as opposed to the hyperbolic (and widely reported) accompanying statements? Those findings—even taken at face value—do not provide a risk-based rationale for highly intrusive smoking bans. The report concludes that chronic ETS exposure increases the risks of lung cancer and heart disease by 20 to 30 percent. While those numbers sound fairly large, one must remember that the underlying risks of lung cancer and heart disease in nonsmokers are quite small to begin with. A 20 percent increase in a tiny risk is, well, really tiny—certainly too tiny to justify the substantial liberty infringement involved in smoking bans. Indeed, risk alone has not justified a ban on smoking itself, an activity that increases the risk of heart disease by 100 to 300 percent and that of lung cancer by 900 percent. How, then, could a much smaller risk justify highly intrusive regulation of the voluntary actions of individuals gathered on private property?

"Secondhand smoke," cartoon by Angel Boligan, Best of Latin America, Cagle Cartoons, El Universal, Mexico City, January 11, 2008. Copyright © Angel Boligan, Cagle Cartoons, El Universal, Mexico City. All rights reserved.

The Underlying Studies

This analysis even assumes that the conclusions of the surgeon general's report are accurate. In fact, they probably are not. The report is a meta-analysis, meaning that the authors did not collect their own epidemiological data but instead combined the results of previously published ETS studies. Meta-analyses are useful analyses, but they are no more compelling than the underlying studies upon which they are based. In this case, the meta-analysis rests on findings from a number of discredited studies, including the 1992 EPA study. Moreover, the analysis treats all studies equally, regardless of their scope and rigor. A number of the underlying studies purporting to document correlations between chronic ETS exposure and cancer or heart disease were quite small, and most employed "case study" methodologies in which individuals with diseases were polled regarding spousal smoking habits or the presence of ETS at their workplaces. A superior study would involve a large number of subjects—some routinely exposed to ETS, some not—and would follow them over time. This sort of "cohort study" is more difficult to perform than after-the-fact case studies, but it is also more accurate.

In fact, an extremely large cohort study has recently been conducted. In 2003, James Enstrom of UCLA and Geoffrey Kabat of the State University of New York, Stony Brook, published a study of the health histories of more than 35,000 never-smoking Californians who were married to smokers. Using information gathered by the American Cancer Society, the researchers collected data on the never-smokers for 39 years (from 1959 to 1998). Their investigation revealed no heightened lung cancer risk among study subjects. In fact, the authors found no "causal relationship between exposure to [ETS] and tobacco-related mortality," though they acknowledged that "a small effect" cannot be ruled out. Enstrom and Kabat's massive study, which has been vociferously criticized by anti-smoking forces, was not even included in the surgeon general's meta-analysis, which covered only studies published through 2002.

A Negligible Risk

The bottom line is that the research on ETS reveals, at most, that even chronic ETS exposure creates only a negligible absolute risk of cancer and heart disease. Advocates of smoking bans must therefore base their risk arguments on non-disease risks.

Some have acknowledged that the purported link between ETS and cancer or heart disease is dubious but have nonetheless maintained that other health risks justify sweeping bans. For example, Dr. Elizabeth Whelan of the pro-ban American Council on Science and Health chastised her fellow ban advocates for "threaten[ing]" their cause with "hyperbole about the likely effects of ETS"—i.e., claims that ETS causes cancer and heart disease. Maintaining that the advocates should have "simply stated that ETS caused irritation of the eyes, nose and respiratory tract and aggravated preexisting asthma," she insisted, that "surely that is enough of a reason to justify the protection of all workers" via a sweeping smoking ban.

Surely it is not. As noted above, paternalistic regulations aimed solely at reducing risks, not at correcting a legitimate market failure, are justifiable only when the risk is relatively serious and the liberty intrusion occasioned by the regulation is relatively minor. Here, the potential harms at issue (a greater number of watery eyes and runny noses, and aggravation of complications among asthmatics who voluntarily patronize establishments where smoking is permitted) do not seem great enough to justify a governmental command that private business owners force their invitees to refrain from an activity that affects only other invitees. Hence, widespread smoking bans are not justifiable solely on risk-based grounds.

EVALUATING THE AUTHORS' ARGUMENTS:

In this viewpoint Lambert notes that smoking itself is not banned even though the risk of disease for smokers is greatly increased. What do you think the three previous authors in this chapter would say to a proposal for a law banning smoking altogether?

Smoking Rates Among Teens in the United States Continue to Decline

University of Michigan News Service

"*Teen smoking reached its recent peak levels around 1996 and 1997, followed by a sharp decline for about six years and a continued more gradual decline ever since.*"

In the following viewpoint the author cites data showing that smoking rates among young people have declined from the recent peak use in 1996. The author indicates that the decline has been due to lower numbers of young people trying cigarettes and less perceived availability. In addition, the author contends that negative social attitudes toward smoking and smokers have helped the decline.

AS YOU READ, CONSIDER THE FOLLOWING QUESTIONS:
  1. According to the author, Monitoring the Future has been con-
    ducting nationwide surveys of U.S. teens for how many years?
  2. What percent of eighth graders in 2009 had tried cigarettes, ac-
    cording to the author?
  3. According to the author, what percent of twelfth graders said they
    would prefer to date people who do not smoke?

Teen smoking reached its recent peak levels around 1996 and 1997, followed by a sharp decline for about six years and a continued more gradual decline ever since, according to the latest Monitoring the Future study of the nation's young people.

"Over the past two years we have seen the smoking rates among young people continue to decline only very gradually, at rates much slower than were occurring previously," said University of Michigan researcher Lloyd Johnston, principal investigator of the Monitoring the Future study. "The proportions of students seeing a great risk associated with being a smoker has leveled off in the past several years, as has the proportion of teens who say they disapprove of smoking."

Monitoring the Future has been conducting annual, nationwide surveys of U.S. teens in school for the past 35 years. The 2009 survey included a total of 46,097 eighth, tenth, and twelfth graders in 389 secondary schools.

The research is conducted by a team of research professors at the University of Michigan's Institute for Social Research, which in addition to Johnston includes Patrick O'Malley, Jerald Bachman, and John Schulenberg. The National Institute on Drug Abuse supports this investigator-initiated study through a series of competitive research grants.

Progress in Teen Smoking Rates

"While great strides have been made in reducing youth smoking in this country, there is still plenty of room for improvement," Johnston said. "Among high school seniors in the Class of 2009, 20 percent have smoked in the most recent month and one in nine (11 percent)

Trends in Prevalence of Cigarette Use for 8th-, 10th-, and 12th-Graders

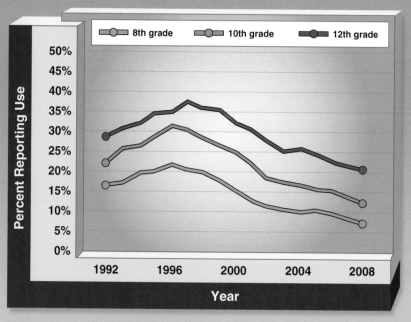

Percentage of Students Using Cigarettes Over a 30-Day Period, 1992–2008

Taken from: University of Michigan, 2008 Monitoring the Future Survey.

is a current daily smoker. Further, our follow-up studies have shown that a number of the lighter smokers in high school will convert to heavy smoking after leaving high school. Given what we know about the consequences of smoking, this is still an unacceptable level of involvement."

To illustrate the progress that has occurred, among 8th graders (13–14-year-olds), the proportion saying that they smoked any cigarettes in the month prior to the survey has dropped by two thirds (from 21 percent in 1996, the peak year, to 7 percent by 2009). Among 10th graders the decline over the same 13-year interval was more than one half (down from 30 percent to 13 percent); among 12th graders, whose smoking rate reached a recent peak in 1997, there has been a decline of almost one half (down from 37 percent in 1997 to 20 percent by 2009). Daily smoking has declined by even larger proportions.

One reason smoking has declined so sharply is that the proportion of students ever *trying smoking* has fallen dramatically. While 49 percent of 8th graders in 1996 had tried cigarettes, "only" 20 percent of the 8th graders in 2009 indicated having ever done so, a decline of six tenths in smoking initiation over the past 13 years.

"These are very substantial improvements in the situation and they have enormous implications for the health and longevity of this newest generation of young Americans," Johnston said.

Slower Progress in Recent Years

But the improvement has been continuing at a much slower rate; over the past two years (2007–2009), the prevalence of smoking in the 30 days prior to the survey has fallen by just 0.6, 0.9, and 1.5 percentage points among 8th, 10th, and 12th graders, respectively.

This reduced rate of improvement, plus the fact that the rises in perceived risk and disapproval of smoking have leveled off, leaves Johnston less optimistic about future gains.

Although there has been a decline in teen smoking, improvement levels have stalled over the last few years.

"Future progress, if it occurs, is likely to be due to changes in the external environment—policy changes such as increasing cigarette taxes, further limiting where smoking is permitted, broad-based prevention campaigns, and making quit-smoking programs more available," Johnston added.

The *perceived availability* of cigarettes to under-age buyers, as measured by the percent of students who say they could buy cigarettes "fairly easily" or "very easily" if they wanted some, has declined substantially since 1996 among 8th and 10th graders (12th graders are not asked the question).

The 8th graders showed the sharpest decline—from 77 percent in 1996 to 56 percent in 2007—about where it remained in 2009. Perceived availability leveled among 10th graders in 2009, having fallen from 91 percent in 1996 to 76 percent by 2009. Although availability has decreased, the investigators note that the majority of these students in their early to mid-teens still report that they could easily get cigarettes.

Attitudes Toward Smoking

A number of attitudes toward smoking and smokers changed in important ways during the period of decline in cigarette use. These changes included increases in preferring to date nonsmokers, strongly disliking being around people who are smoking, thinking that becoming a smoker reflects poor judgment, and believing that smoking is a dirty habit. All of these negative attitudes about smoking and smokers rose to high levels by 2007, but have shown little change since then.

FAST FACT

In 2009 the U.S. Food and Drug Administration banned the sale of flavored cigarettes (except menthol-flavored) in an attempt to deter smoking by young people.

One attitude widely held by young people today may be of particular salience to those considering smoking. In 2009, 81 percent of 8th graders, 80 percent of 10th graders, and 75 percent of 12th graders said that they "would prefer to date people who don't smoke."

It is clear that any young person today who becomes a smoker will pay an important social price for that choice by becoming less attractive to the great majority of the opposite sex.

"This fact provides what we believe could be a very strong prevention message," Johnston said.

EVALUATING THE AUTHOR'S ARGUMENTS:

In this viewpoint the author explains that teen smoking declined sharply between 1996 and 2009. According to the data the author cites, should such sharp declines be expected for the thirteen years following 2009?

Viewpoint 6

Smoking Trends Among Adults Vary by Education and Race

Shanta R. Dube, K. Asman, A. Malarcher, and R. Carabollo

"Overall smoking prevalence did not change significantly from 2007 to 2008."

In the following viewpoint, Shanta R. Dube, K. Asman, A. Malarcher, and R. Carabollo contend that a 2008 health survey questionnaire shows that the rate of adult smokers stayed relatively stable from 2007 to 2008, increasing slightly. In reviewing the demographics of smokers, the authors point to differences in gender, race/ethnicity, and education level of smokers. Dube, Asman, Malarcher, and Carabollo are researchers in the Office on Smoking and Health, part of the National Center for Chronic Disease Prevention and Health Promotion within the U.S. Centers for Disease Control and Prevention.

Shanta R. Dube, K. Asman, A. Malarcher, and R. Carabollo, "Cigarette Smoking Among Adults and Trends in Smoking Cessation—United States, 2008," *Morbidity and Mortality Weekly Report (MMWR)*, vol. 58, November 13, 2009, pp. 1227–1230. Reproduced by permission.

C igarette smoking continues to be the leading cause of preventable morbidity and mortality in the United States. Full implementation of population-based strategies and clinical interventions can educate adult smokers about the dangers of tobacco use and assist them in quitting. To assess progress toward the *Healthy People 2010* objective of reducing the prevalence of cigarette smoking among adults to ≤12%, CDC [Centers for Disease Control and Prevention] analyzed data from the 2008 National Health Interview Survey (NHIS). This report summarizes the results of that analysis, which indicated that during 1998–2008, the proportion of U.S. adults who were current cigarette

> **FAST FACT**
>
> Since 2002, the number of former smokers in the United States has been higher than the number of current smokers.

smokers declined 3.5% (from 24.1% to 20.6%). However, the proportion did not change significantly from 2007 (19.8%) to 2008 (20.6%). In 2008, adults aged ≥25 years with low educational attainment had the highest prevalence of smoking (41.3%) among persons with a General Educational Development certificate [GED] and 27.5% among persons with less than a high school diploma, compared with 5.7% among those with a graduate degree). Adults with education levels at or below the equivalent of a high school diploma, who comprise approximately half of current smokers, had the lowest quit ratios (2008 range: 39.9% to 48.8%). Evidence-based programs known to be effective at reducing smoking should be intensified among groups with lower education, and health-care providers should take education level into account when communicating about smoking hazards and cessation to these patients.

The Smoking Survey

The 2008 NHIS adult core questionnaire was administered by in-person interview and included 21,781 persons aged ≥18 years from among the noninstitutionalized, U.S. civilian population. Respondents were selected by a random probability sample, and the survey included questions on cigarette smoking and cessation attempts. The overall response rate for the 2008 adult core questionnaire was 62.6%. To determine smoking status, respondents were asked, "Have you smoked at least 100 cigarettes in your entire life?" Those who answered "yes" were asked, "Do you now smoke cigarettes every day, some days, or not at all?" Ever smokers were defined as those who reported having smoked at least 100 cigarettes during their lifetime. Current smokers were those who had smoked at least 100 cigarettes during their lifetime and, at the time of interview, reported smoking

It has been reported that smoking is more prevalent among Alaskan Natives and American Indians compared to other racial/ethnic groups.

every day or some days. Former smokers were those who reported smoking at least 100 cigarettes during their lifetime but currently did not smoke. Never smokers were those who reported never having smoked 100 cigarettes during their lifetime. Starting in 2007, income-related follow-up questions were added to NHIS to reduce the number of responses with unknown values. For this report, poverty status was defined by using 2006 poverty thresholds published by the U.S. Census Bureau for the 2007 estimates and 2007 poverty thresholds published by the U.S. Census Bureau for the 2008 estimates; family income was reported by the family respondent who might or might not have been the same as the sample adult respondent from whom smoking information was collected.

To measure trends in cigarette smoking cessation in the population, quit ratios were calculated as the ratio of former smokers to ever smokers for each survey year from 1998 to 2008. Quit ratios were analyzed by education level to determine if differing quit ratios accounted for part of the differing prevalence among education groups. Data were adjusted for nonresponse and weighted to provide national estimates of cigarette smoking prevalence. . . .

Demographics of Smokers

Overall smoking prevalence did not change significantly from 2007 to 2008. In 2008, an estimated 20.6% (46.0 million) of U.S. adults were current cigarette smokers; of these, 79.8% (36.7 million) smoked every day, and 20.2% (9.3 million) smoked some days. Among current cigarette smokers, an estimated 45.3% (20.8 million) had stopped smoking for 1 day or more during the preceding 12 months because they were trying to quit. Of the estimated 94 million persons who had smoked at least 100 cigarettes during their lifetime (ever smokers), 51.1% (48.1 million) were no longer smoking at the time of interview (former smoker).

In 2008, smoking prevalence was higher among men (23.1%) than women (18.3%). Among racial/ethnic groups, Asians had the lowest prevalence (9.9%), and Hispanics had a lower prevalence of smoking (15.8%) than non-Hispanic blacks (21.3%) and non-Hispanic whites (22.0%). American Indians/Alaska Natives had higher prevalence of current smoking compared with the other racial/ethnic groups (32.4%).

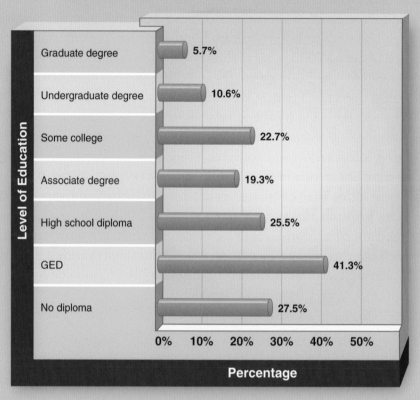

Current Cigarette Smokers by Level of Education, 2008

Level of Education

- Graduate degree — 5.7%
- Undergraduate degree — 10.6%
- Some college — 22.7%
- Associate degree — 19.3%
- High school diploma — 25.5%
- GED — 41.3%
- No diploma — 27.5%

Percentage: 0% 10% 20% 30% 40% 50%

Taken from: Shanta R. Dube, K. Asman, A. Malarcher, and R. Carabollo, "Cigarette Smoking Among Adults and Trends in Smoking Cessation–United States, 2008" *Morbidity and Mortality Weekly Report* (*MMWR*), vol. 58, no. 44, November 13, 2009, p. 1229.

Smoking and Education

Variations in smoking prevalence in 2008 also were observed by education level. Smoking prevalence was highest among adults who had earned a General Education Development certificate (GED). Smoking prevalence was lowest among adults with a graduate degree (5.7%). The prevalence of current smoking was higher among adults living below the federal poverty level (31.5%) than among those at or above this level (19.6%). Smoking prevalence did not vary significantly for adults aged 18–24 years (21.4%), 25–44 years (23.7%), and 45–64 years (22.6%); however, smoking prevalence was lower for adults aged ≥65 years (9.3%).

During 1998–2008, the proportion of U.S. adults who were current cigarette smokers declined 3.5% (from 24.1% to 20.6%), and a statistically significant downward trend was observed. In 2008, quit ratios were lower for adults aged ≥25 years with a GED (39.9%), adults with no high school diploma (45.7%), and adults with a high school diploma (48.8%), compared with quit ratios observed overall for adults aged ≥25 years (53.8%). During 1998–2008, the overall quit ratio was stable (or varied little) and ranged from 48.7% (1998) to 51.1% (2008). Persons with an undergraduate degree and persons with a graduate degree had quit ratios consistently higher than 60.0%. The only group with a significant upward linear trend in cessation was persons with a graduate degree; in 2008, the quit ratio was 80.7%, compared with 76.0% in 1998. Adults with a GED had the lowest quit ratio; during 1998–2008, their quit ratios ranged from 31.2% (2001) to 39.9% (2008).

EVALUATING THE AUTHORS' ARGUMENTS:

In this viewpoint Shanta R. Dube, K. Asman, A. Malarcher, and R. Carabollo assess recent statistics about adult smoking. Comparing their data with that of the previous viewpoint, in what way are teen and adult smoking rates similar in the United States and in what way do they differ?

Chapter 2

What Legal Restrictions Should Be Placed on Smoking?

A variety of restrictions and bans are placed on smoking. This sign restricts smoking in an outdoor location to a certain distance from a specific building.

No Smoking Beyond this Point

Viewpoint
1

Smoking Tobacco Should Be Illegal

John W. Whitehead

"Smoking tobacco should be outlawed, clear and simple."

In the following viewpoint John W. Whitehead argues that tobacco is the most dangerous drug in the United States. He laments the fact that despite the federal government's own studies showing the serious health harms and deaths caused by smoking, no attempt is made to curtail tobacco smoking. Whitehead contends that Congress's inaction is due to the political contributions of the tobacco industry. He concludes that the only reasonable policy on tobacco in the smoked form is to outlaw it. Whitehead is an attorney and founder of the Rutherford Institute, a nonprofit civil liberties and human rights organization.

1. According to the author, what is the yearly economic toll of smoking in the United States?
2. How much did the tobacco industry spend to lobby Congress in 2003, according to Whitehead?
3. According to Whitehead, what percent of smokers begin at or before age eighteen?

Every day, the U.S. government spends millions of dollars in its efforts to prevent illegal drugs from entering this country. The [George W.] Bush Administration even has a spirited campaign against marijuana, going so far as to fight medicinal marijuana use and any product that may have a trace of hemp in it. However, while the most frightful and dangerous drug on the planet rages in the bodies of millions of Americans, including a large segment of our young people, our government is doing virtually nothing to stop it.

Smoking and Health

Indeed, the U.S. Surgeon General has recently released a comprehensive report on smoking and health. It reveals for the first time that smoking causes diseases in nearly every organ of the human body. Published 40 years after the Surgeon General's first report on smoking —which concluded that smoking was a definite cause of three serious diseases (lung and larynx cancer and chronic bronchitis)—this newest report finds that cigarette smoking is conclusively linked to diseases such as leukemia, cataracts, pneumonia and cancers of the cervix, kidney, pancreas and stomach.

According to this new report, smoking kills an estimated 440,000 Americans each year. On average, men who smoke cut their lives short by 13.2 years, and female smokers lose 14.5 years. The economic toll exceeds $157 billion each year in the United States—$75 billion in direct medical costs and $82 billion in lost productivity.

Statistics indicate that more than 12 million Americans have died from smoking since the 1964 report of the Surgeon General. Moreover, another 25 million Americans alive today will most likely die of smoking-related illnesses. And it doesn't matter what type of cigarette is smoked. In fact, another major conclusion from the latest report, consistent with recent findings of other scientific studies, is that smoking so-called low-tar or low-nicotine cigarettes does not offer any health benefits over smoking regular or "full-flavor" cigarettes. "There is no safe cigarette, whether it is called 'light,' 'ultra-light' or any other name," the Surgeon General has said. "The science is clear: the only way to avoid the health hazards of smoking is to quit completely or to never start smoking."

The Impact of Political Contributions

The obvious question is: If tobacco is the most lethal and dangerous drug in the United States, why is it not greatly curtailed or even made illegal? To find the answer, one need look no further than political contributions.

The tobacco industry has made more than $1.8 million in political contributions to federal candidates, political parties and political committees so far in 2003–2004. And, according to a quarterly report issued by the Campaign for Tobacco-Free Kids Action Fund and Common Cause, since 1997, the tobacco industry has contributed more than $27.7 million

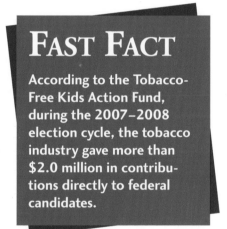

FAST FACT

According to the Tobacco-Free Kids Action Fund, during the 2007–2008 election cycle, the tobacco industry gave more than $2.0 million in contributions directly to federal candidates.

to various political action committees. And since 1999, tobacco companies have also spent more than $101 million on lobbying the U.S. Congress. Indeed, the tobacco industry spent more than $21.2 million to lobby Congress in 2003. That amounts to approximately $127,000 spent on lobbying for every day that Congress was in session.

The report from the Campaign for Tobacco-Free Kids Action Fund demonstrates how the tobacco industry's contributions are used to thwart public health policy. The report details contributions to the sponsors and co-sponsors of legislation that would provide for regulation of tobacco products by the Food and Drug Administration. In

William V. Corr, during his term as executive director of the Campaign for Tobacco-Free Kids Action Fund, released a report detailing contributions of tobacco companies to politcal action committees and funds spent by them to lobby Congress to thwart anti-tobacco legislation.

fact, the 17 House members who sponsored legislation opposed by the public health industry received, on average, more than 20 times as much money from the tobacco industry than the 127 sponsors of public health–conscious legislation.

A Harmful Silence

One is tempted to argue that the lobbying process as used by the tobacco companies is democracy in action. However, at base it is the rawest form of political corruption when big money buys the loyalty of members of Congress and forces a nefarious silence from our president and other political leaders. As William V. Corr, executive director of the Campaign for Tobacco-Free Kids Action Fund, said when releasing his study, "Today's report tells us why there has been so little action on tobacco in Congress, despite the fact that more than 2,000 kids become addicted smokers every day and more than 400,000 Americans die every year from tobacco use."

Sadly, nearly 90 percent of smokers begin at or before age 18. Those

Lobbying Expenditures of the Five Biggest Spenders in the Tobacco Industry, 1999–2006

	Tobacco Company				
Year	Altria/Philip Morris	Lorillard	Brown & Williamson	RJ Reynolds	U.S. Smokeless Tobacco Co.
1999	$14,720,000	$1,060,000	$2,330,000	$1,519,320	$1,020,000
2000	$11,220,000	$1,500,000	$2,460,000	$1,365,525	$940,000
2001	$12,520,000	$1,980,000	$1,560,000	$1,333,380	$1,200,000
2002	$14,040,000	$1,840,000	$1,600,000	$1,290,450	$1,460,000
2003	$13,480,000	$2,360,000	$1,880,000	$1,531,135	$1,700,000
2004	$13,240,000	$2,880,000	$1,060,000	$1,678,030	$1,840,000
2005	$13,640,000	$1,940,000	$0	$1,739,100	$1,238,000
2006	$12,840,000	$1,200,000	$0	$767,360	$1,640,000
Total	$105,700,000	$14,760,000	$10,890,000	$11,224,720	$11,038,000

Taken from: Tobacco-Free Kids and Common Cause, "Campaign Contributors by Tobacco Interests," Annual Report, September 2007.

who peddle the death that is tobacco target young smokers in the hopes of hooking human beings on tobacco for the rest of their lives. And as we're finding, the only outcome is sickness and death.

So, what should be done? Smoking tobacco should be outlawed, clear and simple. Why would we settle for anything less?

EVALUATING THE AUTHORS' ARGUMENTS:

In this viewpoint Whitehead argues that smoking tobacco should be outlawed. Why does Ethan Nadelmann, author of the next viewpoint, disagree?

Smoking Tobacco Should Not Be Illegal

Ethan Nadelmann

"Prohibition can not, and must not, be the end result of today's vigorous anti-smoking campaign."

In the following viewpoint Ethan Nadelmann argues that prohibition of cigarettes should be avoided. Citing the results of a recent poll, Nadelmann worries that more and more people will begin to back a movement to make cigarettes illegal. Despite all the gains in health that a prohibition on smoking would bring, he argues that these would be offset by the harms caused by illicit tobacco production, distribution, and use. Nadelmann is the founder and executive director of the Drug Policy Alliance, an organization that promotes alternatives to the war on drugs.

Ethan Nadelmann, "Keep Cigarettes Legal," *Huffington Post*, October 26, 2006. Reproduced by permission of the author.

Would you support a federal law making cigarettes illegal in the next five to ten years? According to a recent nationwide survey of registered voters by Zogby International, 45% of Americans said yes. Among 18–29 year olds, 57% were in favor.

Maybe it's time to ask: what if cigarettes became the new Prohibition?

The New Prohibition

The upside is clear. Millions of American smokers would finally quit, and millions more would never start. Smoking-related death and disease would drop significantly. That's all to the good, but it's not all that would happen.

Millions of Americans, perhaps tens of millions, would keep puffing. Big tobacco wouldn't disappear; it would just change hands and go underground, discarding its high priced lobbyists in favor of people more skilled in violence and intimidation. Some tobacco farmers would find other work but thousands more would become outlaws, producing their crops covertly. Mexico's and Colombia's narco-traficantes would rejoice at the opportunities for new markets and profits. "Tobacco-related murders" would increase dramatically as criminal organizations competed with one another for turf and markets, and ordinary crime would skyrocket as millions of tobacco junkies sought ways to feed their costly addiction. Smoking would become an act of youthful rebellion; no doubt some users would begin to experiment with even more dangerous forms of tobacco. Fewer people would die in their sixties of cancer and emphysema, but more would die young from the harms and life style associated with illicit tobacco addiction.

And just imagine the government's "war on tobacco": hundreds of thousands of new jobs for federal, state and local police, and hundreds of thousands of new prison cells for tobacco producers, pushers and users; government helicopters spraying herbicides on illicit tobacco fields here and abroad; people rewarded for informing on tobacco-growing, -selling, and -smoking neighbors; police seizing the cars of people caught smoking; urine tests commonplace to identify users; tobacco courts compelling addicts to quit or go to jail; and an ever bigger federal police agency—the Tobacco Enforcement Administration (the T.E.A.)—employing undercover agents, informants, and wire-taps to get the bad guys. Forget, too, about the twenty-plus

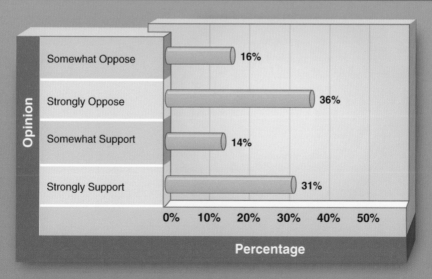

Should Cigarettes Be Illegal?

This graph shows the results of the following question in a 2006 Zogby poll:

"Would you strongly support, somewhat support, somewhat oppose, or strongly oppose a federal law making cigarettes illegal within the next five to ten years?"

Somewhat Oppose 16%

Strongly Oppose 36%

Somewhat Support 14%

Strongly Support 31%

Opinion

0% 10% 20% 30% 40% 50%

Percentage

Taken from: Zogby poll, "Federal Ban on Cigarettes?" Drug Policy Alliance, July 2006
[http://www.drugpolicy.org/docUploads/DPAZogbyTobaccoPoll2006.pdf].

billion dollars per year in tobacco taxes earned by the federal and state governments prior to prohibition. The new "tax collectors" would be organized and unorganized criminals, even as governments spent tens of billions per year trying futilely to enforce the new Prohibition.

The Increasing Intolerance of Nonsmokers

Is such a scenario improbable? I think not, given our country's rich history of enacting prohibitions with little foresight or forethought. Drug prohibitions tend to be embraced not when a drug is most popular but rather when use is declining, and increasingly concentrated among people who are poorer, darker and younger.

Proprietor and anti-smoking ban activist Armando Frallicciardi Jr. smokes with others at his restaurant, Lorenzo's, in New Jersey. Frallicciardi along with a coalition of bars, restaurants, and bowling alleys filed a lawsuit in March 2006, claiming the ban on smoking in indoor places in New Jersey was unconstitutional.

As the number of smokers drops, the dangerous logic of prohibition becomes ever more tempting. Forty years ago, when half of all men and a third of all women smoked, most non-smokers barely noticed cigarette smoke unless it was particularly thick or right in their face. Now, with barely one in five Americans still smoking, we non-smokers are increasingly intolerant. We think smoking cigarettes is filthy, deadly and offensive. We've become accustomed to bans on smoking—by minors, and in more and more workplaces and public spaces—and on advertising cigarettes. And we hate the corporations that profit off this deadly product.

But it's important not to get carried away with our rhetoric and our bans. Stigmatizing smokers and smoking persuades some to stop and deters others from starting, but demonizing and dehumanizing those who persist is both morally wrong and dangerous. The ever higher taxes and broader bans on cigarettes have played an important role in reducing both the number of smokers and the amount they smoke. Persisting with these policies will no doubt lead to further reductions. But there is a point of declining returns at which the costs of such policies begin to outweigh the benefits.

> **FAST FACT**
>
> In 2004, it became illegal to smoke in public or sell tobacco in the country of Bhutan, a nation in South Asia of approximately 700,000 people.

The Anti-Smoking Campaign

Why sound the alarm before the fire's begun? Because those poll results suggest that millions of Americans just aren't thinking through the consequences of making cigarettes entirely illegal.

Now's the time for anti-smoking advocates, public health leaders—and police chiefs—to affirm that prohibition can not, and must not, be the end result of today's vigorous anti-smoking campaign—even if the number of smokers drops from today's forty million to less than ten million. Ditto for [New York] Mayor [Michael] Bloomberg, given his political and very generous philanthropic commitment to the cause of reducing smoking.

And, full disclosure: I hate cigarettes. I don't like the smell. I don't like the look. And I don't like the fact that my dad's pack-a-day habit no doubt contributed to the massive heart attack that killed him at 58. My teenage daughter knows there are few things she could do that would upset me more than to start smoking cigarettes.

But a new Prohibition is not the answer—not if we want to stay safe, sane and free.

EVALUATING THE AUTHORS' ARGUMENTS:

In this viewpoint Nadelmann argues that it is a bad idea to outlaw cigarettes because of the harms of prohibition. Do you think that John W. Whitehead, author of the preceding viewpoint, would argue that the harms of legal cigarettes are worse than the harms of making cigarettes illegal? What evidence might he use in his argument?

Smoking Should Be Banned in Bars and Restaurants

Milwaukee Journal Sentinel

"It's simply unworthy of us as a state to make workers choose between a paycheck and bad health."

In the following viewpoint the *Milwaukee Journal Sentinel* argues that it is right for Wisconsin to enact a statewide smoking ban in bars and restaurants. The author claims that the rights of workers to health trumps the right of business owners to allow smoking at their place of business. Although the bill contains some compromises, the author claims these are reasonable. As far as arguments against the ban, including the notion that it represents excessive government intrusion, the author asserts that the government has an obligation to keep its citizens safe. The *Milwaukee Journal Sentinel* is a daily newspaper in Milwaukee, Wisconsin.

AS YOU READ, CONSIDER THE FOLLOWING QUESTIONS:
  1. What three other Midwest states already enacted statewide smoking bans, according to the author?
  2. According to the *Milwaukee Journal Sentinel*, how long is the phase-in period for the smoking ban?
  3. The author disputes the worry about nanny-state intrusion by implying that the government's job is to do what?

B reathe easier. Unless some poison-pill amendment garners support on the Legislature's floor, it appears Wisconsin will cease being the ashtray of the Midwest. A statewide smoking ban could be enacted as early as Wednesday.

Minnesota, Illinois and Iowa, hands on hips, can quit sniffing at Wisconsin's stinky clothes, saying, "And where have you been?" The more pertinent question, anyway: "How come it's taken you so long to get home?"

The compromise worked out last week by supporters of a statewide smoking ban, the Tavern League of Wisconsin, restaurant interests and legislative leaders is far from perfect. Still, it and the fast track that will give it floor votes in both houses this week deserve broad support.

Fast tracked?

It seems as though Wisconsinites have been holding their breaths over this one for far too long. Other states and entire nations have recognized that the health of its citizens trumps anyone's alleged "right" to threaten the health of workers and patrons. But, as with its drunken driving laws, Wisconsin has contented itself being dangerously different.

It's clear that the governor's inclusion of the ban in his budget forced some hands. As part of the budget bill, the governor had the votes on the Joint Finance Committee, and this was enough to compel folks to sit at the table in good faith.

And opponents also were likely eyeing the Democratic majorities in both houses, which spelled success for a ban even as a stand-alone bill. And its emergence from an Assembly committee on Friday on a bipartisan 11–2 vote indicates this bill indeed has legs. All of this likely contributed to a sense of urgency among opponents—deal or have no voice. And also out there is the governor's veto powers. A compromise is better insurance that he now won't line out items to make the ban even more stringent.

The Joint Finance Committee deserves credit for taking the ban out of the budget and the governor credit both for not resisting this and for making a smoking ban one of his signature issues. . . .

Senate Majority Leader Russ Decker (D-Weston) came around, even reportedly pushing for a resolution. Why?

The governor's inclusion of the ban in his budget, of course, but it would not surprise us if Decker simply figured the political calculus and

President Barack Obama meets with Governor Jim Doyle of Wisconsin and Governor Jennifer Granholm of Michigan. Both states have included smoking bans in their budgets as a result of health-care discussions with the president and vice president. Wisconsin is the last midwestern state to enlist such a ban.

was unwilling to continue being the fall guy for the Legislature's failure to enact a ban. Frankly, the reason doesn't much matter. If he pushed for a resolution, he has our thanks.

Blocking this again would have placed him on the wrong side of history and public sentiment. There's a reason about three dozen Wisconsin communities, as the state has refused to act, have enacted their own local bans, making for a patchwork of regulation.

Another likely factor: the departure of one of the statewide ban's most strident opponents, former Democratic Sen. Roger Breske of Eland, from the Legislature. A former Tavern League president, Breske was appointed last year by Gov. Jim Doyle to be the state's railroad commissioner.

Good move, governor. Rep. Jon Richards (D-Milwaukee) and Sen. Fred Risser (D-Madison) also deserve credit for pushing this legislation so strongly.

This time around, the Tavern League read the tea leaves, and smoking ban supporters realized that holding out for the perfect threatened the good.

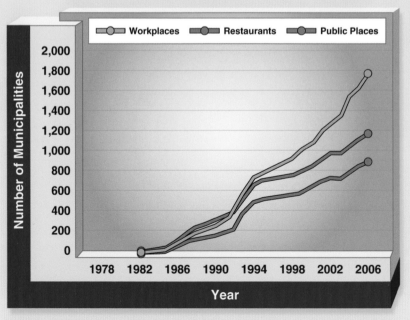

Taken from: U.S. Department of Health & Human Services, "The Health Consequences of Involuntary Exposure to Tobacco Smoke: A Report of the Surgeon General," 2006.

That's what this compromise is: merely good, not perfect.

The roughly one-year phase-in period for taverns and restaurants is one more year in which the health of workers and patrons is harmed.

Yes, an immediate ban would have no doubt resulted in the immediate loss of some bar and restaurant patrons who smoke. But it's unlikely these folks will quit eating out or drinking in taverns for long.

A phase-in period was a necessary compromise. Wisconsinites will get a smoking ban. That's the important thing.

Exempting cigar bars and smoke shops is only fair. They are, after all, about tobacco.

The fines—and the fact there is no enforcement money in this bill—strike us as lenient but worth conceding to get to a statewide ban. Bar owners will not be penalized if they've attempted to stop the smoker or on a first offense. They could, however, be fined $100 for subsequent offenses.

Bars and restaurants also will be able to establish outdoor dining and drinking areas for smokers. One lapse in this regard, however. A better bill would allow hotels to set aside a portion of their rooms for smokers. This, too, is a matter of fairness.

Should some legislator out there be contemplating an amendment to torpedo the bill, there are folks aplenty who will argue the point.

Fear that those smokers will permanently disappear as clientele? Bruno Johnson and his wife own two bars, The Palm and The Sugar Maple, both in Bay View, both nonsmoking. The math was simple. "The majority of people don't smoke," he said. Another rationale, aside from his family living above one of his bars, for going smoke-free: He sells higher-end beers and prefers that his patrons be able to taste them.

Shawn Lange owns Boz's Sports Bar and Grill in West Allis, and he stresses the health aspect. He has a kid. "I'd like to be around a bit longer." Since he quit smoking, the smoking of others conspired against that.

And Kim Zick, better known as part of the musical group Mrs. Fun, said this in a letter to legislators: "Musicians and all bar and restaurant employees are entitled to a smoke-free workplace. . . . The majority of workers in the United States work in a clean, healthy workplace, which should be afforded to all working citizens."

There is, of course, the argument of nanny-state intrusion. Well, only if the government's job isn't to keep its citizens reasonably safe. Not buying it? Fine. Let's bring back asbestos. Funny how banning gay marriage is not nanny-state in small-government circles, but keeping people healthy is.

And it's simply unworthy of us as a state to make workers choose between a paycheck and bad health.

The slippery-slope argument doesn't wash, either. Next, goes the argument, will come smoking bans in homes and cars. True, small children cannot protect themselves from smoking parents, but such a ban is unlikely to happen. Any scare tactic will do, however.

It's time. The state Legislature this week should enact this compromise on a statewide smoking ban, and the governor should sign it.

EVALUATING THE AUTHOR'S ARGUMENTS:

In this viewpoint the *Milwaukee Journal Sentinel* contends that workers in bars and restaurants will be protected by a statewide smoking ban. The author raises several of the points made by those opposing the smoking ban. Does this strengthen or weaken the author's argument?

Smoking Should Not Be Banned in Bars and Restaurants

Yvonne Angieri

"It is clear to many people that a smoking ban would be an unnecessary and intrusive measure, one that would achieve the opposite of its original intent."

In the following viewpoint Yvonne Angieri argues that a proposed smoking ban in bars and restaurants in St. Louis, Missouri, is misguided. Angieri believes that private business owners should be able to allow smoking if they want, and that air filtration systems are a good way to protect workers and patrons in smoking establishments. Angieri contends that although the intent of the ban is to protect workers, it actually will end up harming them because it will lead to a loss of revenue for many businesses, and therefore the threat of lost employment, benefits, and wages. Angieri is a St. Louis University student who manages two restaurants in St. Louis.

AS YOU READ, CONSIDER THE FOLLOWING QUESTIONS:
  1. Angieri cites a study published in 2003 in the *British Medical Journal*; what conclusion did that study reach?
  2. The author claims that employers already can provide clean air to their employees of smoking establishments by doing what?
  3. Angieri claims that a smoking ban in Columbia, Missouri, caused bar revenues to decrease by what percent?

The ongoing national debate regarding the relative merits of banning smoking in restaurants and bars has sparked a great deal of controversy here in St. Louis as the issue has come closer to home. This issue interests me personally because, in addition to attending St. Louis University as a full-time undergraduate student, I also am a manager at two of St. Louis' finest restaurants: Monarch Restaurant in Maplewood and Herbie's Vintage '72 in the Central West End.

Public Smoking and Public Health

I am not a smoker, nor do I care for the smell of smoke. But I do believe that private property owners should be trusted with the choice of whether to offer either a smoke-free or a smoking environment in their own establishments to their own clientele.

FAST FACT

Residents of St. Louis County, Missouri, approved a referendum on November 4, 2009, that bans smoking beginning in 2011, exempting casinos and certain bars.

Neither do I wish to be depicted as "anti-health" or "anti-progress." But couching the issue of "public" smoking solely in terms of public health is misleading.

I recently learned that the Occupational Safety and Health Administration itself has refused to impose a strict ban, as proposed by St. Louis Alderman Lyda Krewson, D-28th Ward. Furthermore, studies on exposure to secondhand smoke produce very mixed results. A 2003 study by epidemiologists James Enstrom and Geoffrey Kabat, published in the *British Medical Journal*, found no evidence that secondhand smoke causes lung cancer or heart disease. A recent multi-state study by RAND, the Congressional Budget Office and University of Wisconsin and Stanford University researchers found no link between smoking bans and a reduction of heart attacks or other serious diseases.

The Option of Air Filtration

Besides, employers already have a means of providing clean indoor air for employees and patrons alike: air filtration. When Herbie's Vintage '72 opened in October, the owners installed air filtration systems in both the bar and private cigar lounge. I was pleasantly surprised by their effectiveness. After a busy night, I leave the restaurant with virtually no smell of smoke in my hair or my clothes.

The elimination of this irritation prompted me to re-evaluate my opinion of air filtration. While legal concerns keep filtration manufacturers from making health claims, their technical specifications

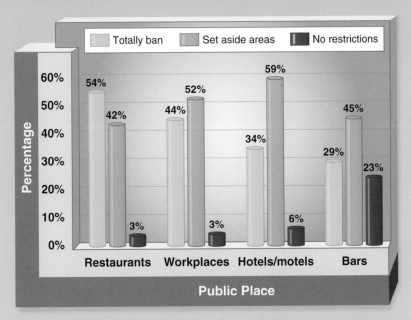

Opinions on Smoking in Public Places

Taken from: Gallup poll, July 12–15, 2007 [http://www.gallup.com/poll/2816/More-Smokers-Feeling-Harassed-Smoking-Bans.aspx].

demonstrate that their machines not only are highly effective in making indoor air cleaner than outdoor air, but they also filter out such threats as swine or avian flu viruses.

The owner of a private establishment, a "house" if you will, should have the right to offer his guests a place to smoke and to choose the most effective means of cleaning the air. Granting establishments the freedom to purify their air using effective modern technology would allow their owners the opportunity to provide a cleaner working environment for employees and achieve a harmonious balance in accommodating both smoking and non-smoking guests—as Herbie's has succeeded in doing.

The Risk to Workers
It also would ensure that employees like me are secure in a workplace that is not in jeopardy because of lost revenue that might result from a smoking ban. Loss of livelihood and medical insurance caused by

This patron smokes a cigarette at a bar in St. Louis on January 23, 2008. Economist Michael R. Pakko says smoking bans can have a detrimental impact to the economics of businesses, especially bars.

closures and cutbacks surely pose a serious and immediate health risk to hospitality employees. This is a real possibility: research by Federal Reserve economists blames the Illinois smoking ban for a 20 percent decline in casino revenues and holds the Columbia, Mo., smoking ban responsible for an 11 percent decrease in bar revenues. For restaurant workers supporting families, these numbers can mean financial ruin and an actual decline in standard of living.

As a manager of a St. Louis city restaurant, I want to know that my interests and those of my colleagues truly are being protected. I am not alone in my concern. St. Louis County Executive Charlie A. Dooley, the Missouri Restaurant Association and the Independent Restaurant and Tavern Owners Association of Greater St. Louis all have opposed a city and county smoking ban in order to avert the grave potential economic damage of such a restriction.

It is clear to many people that a smoking ban would be an unnecessary and intrusive measure, one that would achieve the opposite of its original intent. Instead of protecting workers, it would hurt them. Government exists to safeguard the lives, freedom and self-determination of its citizens. St. Louis would thus do well to live up to its good name and look out for all its citizens. [A partial smoking ban was passed in St. Louis in 2009.]

EVALUATING THE AUTHORS' ARGUMENTS:

In this viewpoint, Angieri claims that air filtration is an alternative to smoking bans. How do you think the other authors in this chapter would respond to her proposal? Explain.

Viewpoint 5

Smoking Bans in Outdoor Public Places Make Sense

John Banzhaf

> *"Concentrations of secondhand tobacco smoke in many outdoor areas are often as high or higher than in some indoor areas."*

In the following viewpoint John Banzhaf argues that there are many reasons for banning smoking in outdoor areas. Banzhaf claims that secondhand smoke outdoors can lead to health hazards for nonsmokers. In addition, Banzhaf claims that people should not have to suffer annoyance and irritation caused by breathing secondhand smoke. Banzhaf also refers to discarded cigarette butts and the protection of children as justifications for outdoor smoking bans. Banzhaf is a law professor at George Washington University Law School and the founder of Action on Smoking and Health (ASH), a nonprofit antismoking organization.

John Banzhaf, "Reasons for Banning Smoking in Certain Public Outdoor Areas," Action on Smoking and Health (ASH), November 8, 2005. Courtesy of Action on Smoking and Health (ASH).

AS YOU READ, CONSIDER THE FOLLOWING QUESTIONS:
1. According to Banzhaf, how many Americans have chronic conditions such as asthma and bronchitis?
2. Banzhaf claims that cigarette butts are a litter problem in what four outdoor places?
3. How many jurisdictions have already enacted outdoor smoking bans, according to the author?

C areful scientific studies—based upon both highly accurate mathematical modeling techniques as well as actual real-life measurements—have shown that concentrations of secondhand tobacco smoke in many outdoor areas are often as high or higher than in some indoor areas and that the risks posed by such outdoor exposure, while small to most individuals, are well beyond generally accepted norms when large numbers of people are involuntarily exposed. Indeed, for these very reasons, the State of California—in a report summarizing much of this evidence—was preparing and has now declared *OUTDOOR* tobacco smoke as a "toxic air pollutant."

The Health Hazards of Outdoor Smoke

Drifting tobacco smoke, even outdoors, can trigger asthmatic attacks, bronchial infections, and other serious health problems in nonsmokers. This is especially true for the almost 100 million Americans who have asthma, chronic bronchitis, chronic sinusitis, emphysema, and other breathing-related conditions which make them especially susceptible to secondhand tobacco smoke.

Even for people without such respiratory conditions, breathing drifting tobacco smoke for even brief periods can be deadly. For example, the Centers for Disease Controls [CDC] has warned that breathing drifting tobacco smoke for as little as 30 minutes (less than the time one might be exposed outdoors on a beach, sitting on a park bench, listening to a concert in a park, etc.) can raise a nonsmoker's risk of suffering a fatal heart attack to that of a smoker. The danger is even greater for those who are already at an elevated risk for coronary problems: e.g., men over 40 and postmenopausal women, anyone who is obese, has diabetes, a personal or family history of heart or circulatory conditions, gets insufficient exercise, has high blood pressure, cholesterol, etc.

In cases where drifting tobacco smoke was present and a nonsmoker suffered a heart attack, asthmatic attack, or other similar problems, the municipality which owns and operates the beach, park, playground, etc. could be liable since it was on notice of the known health dangers but failed to take the "reasonable" step of banning smoking as taken by many other outdoor areas.

Society recognizes that people have a right not to be involuntarily exposed to known carcinogenic substances, even if only to small amounts and for brief periods. That's why, for example, extensive and very expensive precautions are taken when asbestos is removed from buildings. This insures that people outside are not exposed even to minute amounts as they pass by. Similarly, we would not tolerate someone who filed down old brake drums in a playground, thereby releasing even tiny amounts of asbestos into the air. Secondhand tobacco smoke is officially classified by the federal government as a "known human carcinogen"—exactly the same category as asbestos.

Annoyance and Irritation

Even aside from health hazards, being forced to breathe tobacco smoke is annoying and irritating to most people, especially the almost 100 million Americans who have chronic conditions like asthma and bronchitis which make them especially susceptible to tobacco smoke, and young children who are also especially sensitive. It should be noted that many activities are banned in public places simply because they are annoying or irritating, even if they do not pose a health hazard. Common examples are playing loud music on portable radios or boom boxes, engaging in sexually provocative activity, using profanity, dressing in inappropriately scanty attire, drinking alcoholic beverages, etc.

Many of the 96 million Americans who have chronic conditions like asthma and bronchitis which make them especially susceptible to tobacco smoke have been held to be entitled to protection under the Americans With Disabilities Act [ADA]. Thus, if their medical conditions mean that they cannot enjoy lying on a blanket at the beach or in a park for a concert where smoking is generally permitted, they may be entitled by law to a reasonable accommodation, presumably one which protects them from drifting tobacco smoke.

The reason for banning smoke around building entrances is simple. People should not be forced to be exposed to known carcinogenic substances for even the briefest periods of time, and because even brief exposure can also be annoying and irritating to many people, non-smokers should not be forced to "run a gauntlet" of smokers gathered around the exits and entrances to their workplaces, or other buildings which they are likely to frequent.

Large buildings ordinarily have air intakes to replace the air which is exhausted by their ventilation systems. Occasionally, the air intake will be located near a doorway to the building, or in some other area where smokers might tend to congregate. Therefore, to prevent this smoke-filled air from entering and being circulated throughout the building where it can create a health risk as well as annoyance and physical irritation, it may be necessary to prohibit smoking outdoors around such air intakes.

The Problem of Cigarette Butts

Cigarette butts discarded by smokers constitute the overwhelming majority of litter on beaches, as well as in many other public places like parks, playgrounds, and sidewalks. Smoking bans have been shown to substantially reduce the litter and therefore the costs of cleaning up beaches and other outdoor areas, as well as to improve the overall appearance and attractiveness of the area.

Cigarettes are a major source of burns to youngsters, including to their faces, when smokers hold their cigarettes at their sides and young children inadvertently come too close. This can happen easily when children are at play or otherwise distracted on a beach, waiting on a line while their parents wait to buy tickets, to use ATM machines, etc.—and once again there may be legal liability.

Discarded cigarettes—which are designed to continue to burn for several minutes when dropped and not puffed upon—are also a major fire hazard, threatening piers, boardwalks, and wooden structures in parks and playgrounds, etc., as well as outdoor park and recreation areas.

Young children playing in the sand at a beach or in playground sandbox may be tempted to put cigarette butts—which contain concentrated amounts of carcinogens and other toxic chemicals trapped from tobacco smoke—into their mouths, and even older children may touch the cigarette butts and then put their fingers in or near their mouths, eyes, etc.

Discarded cigarette butts may also be harmful to birds and other wildlife which nibble on or even swallow them, especially on a beach or park, but also even on a public sidewalk. Indeed, one of the first domestic bans on outdoor smoking was enacted to protect wildlife rather than human beings.

A Bad Habit

Activities and images which might be inappropriate for young children and/or which might lead them into bad habits are often prohibited in public places, even if they pose no health risk and might even be appropriate in areas visited voluntarily only by adults. For example, virtually all municipalities have long prohibited consumption of alcoholic beverages in public places like parks and beaches. The purpose is obviously not to prevent drunkenness or driving while intoxicated—since people can easily get drunk drinking in their parked cars, in bars, and at home. Rather, bans are imposed because drinking sets a bad example for young children to see it done openly—even if the same children might see it in their own homes. Similarly, prohibiting smoking in outdoor places frequented by the public—like parks, playgrounds, beaches, etc.—shields young children from seeing smoking as a common adult behavior to be emulated, even if some may observe smoking by the parents and other adults in private homes. Other examples where activities are prohibited in public places because of their possible impact on children include sexually suggestive movements (permitted on dance floors but prohibited in parks and on sidewalks), gambling (permitted in casinos and tracks but not in public places), displays of pictorial nudity (permitted in art galleries but not on sidewalks), etc.

The Great Outdoors. Now Even Greater.

A new law makes common areas in state parks smoke-free. This includes:
• Beaches • Playgrounds • Snack bars • Picnic shelters
• Business facilities • Any enclosed public place or public restroom

For more information visit www.tobaccofreemaine.org

Healthy Maine Partnerships

Crescent Beach State Park in Cape Elizabeth, Maine, distributes cards to visitors informing them of the no-smoking laws at state parks. The 2009 law bars smoking in all outdoor public areas, such as patios and decks, state parks, beaches, playgrounds, snack bars, and group picnic shelters.

In addition to all of the above reasons, it has now become clear that restrictions on smoking are a major factor in helping to persuade smokers to quit, and to help those who want to stop smoking to do so. The result can be an enormous saving of lives, in the prevention of disability, and in a dramatic reduction in health care costs—most of which are borne by nonsmokers who otherwise are forced to pay higher taxes and inflated health insurance premiums. Smoking bans—including outdoors as well as indoors—encourage and support quitting by making it more inconvenient for a person to remain a smoker. Every ban on smoking also sends a very clear educational message to the smoker that his conduct is not desirable—and indeed is found to be annoying and irritating if not repugnant—by a large majority of others. Finally, smoking bans help those already trying to quit by tending to assure that they will not be tempted by being in the presence of a smoker, smell the "tempting" aroma of tobacco smoke, etc.

While not the primary argument or purpose in enacting outdoor smoking bans, this additional significant effect of such bans may well be a factor in deciding to support such public health measures.

Outdoor Smoking Bans

More than 350 jurisdictions have successfully prohibited smoking in outdoor areas—such as beaches, parks, playgrounds, near building entrances, while waiting in lines, etc.—without legal challenges, problems of enforcement, loss of patronage or taxes, etc. Such bans appear to be so successful that more jurisdictions are sure to be added. Indeed, as smoking is being banned in an ever growing number of indoor areas, people are beginning to expect freedom from these toxic fumes, and to expect air unpolluted by tobacco smoke wherever they may congregate.

Very strong recent evidence of this trend is the overwhelming vote by the citizens of the State of Washington to ban smoking not only in all bars and restaurants, but to also require that building entrances be smokefree, and to prohibit smoking within 25 feet of doorways, windows, and ventilation ducts of smokefree establishments. This vote comes on the heels of a poll by the New York State Health Department which showed that the public support for banning smoking in many outdoor areas is even stronger than similar support for a 2003 bill banning indoor smoking.

> **EVALUATING THE AUTHORS' ARGUMENTS:**
>
> In this viewpoint Banzhaf contends that one reason for banning outdoor smoking is that it sets a bad example for children. Why does William Saletan, author of the next viewpoint, reject this justification?

Viewpoint 6

Smoking Bans in Outdoor Public Places Go Too Far

William Saletan

"You don't have to ban smoking on every square inch of park land in order to protect nonsmokers."

In the following viewpoint William Saletan contends that banning smoking outdoors is excessive. Saletan argues that the rationale that applies to indoor smoking bans— the risk of secondhand smoke to nonsmokers—does not apply in large outdoor areas. Saletan claims that there are ways to protect nonsmokers in parks without completely banning smoking. He rejects the justification that smoking should be banned so that children will not see it; he also rejects any need to recognize a value in smoking in order to keep it legal in outdoor spaces. Saletan is national correspondent at Slate.com.

AS YOU READ, CONSIDER THE FOLLOWING QUESTIONS:

1. What two cities does Saletan cite as having already passed outdoor smoking bans?
2. Why does Saletan claim that the secondhand smoke studies do not apply to outdoor spaces?
3. What example of another ban does Saletan give in order to show why the cultural contamination of children is not a good justification for an outdoor smoking ban?

Hey, you! Stop smoking in my atmosphere! That's the message from New York City, where the mayor and health commissioner have just released a policy agenda called "Take Care New York 2012." Page 10 of the document says the city's health department "will work with the city's Department of Parks and Recreation and other entities to expand smoke-free spaces to include city parks and public beaches." The city council speaker is very interested in the idea, but her help might not be necessary if the parks department can implement the ban as a regulation.

According to the *New York Post*, cities and counties in Utah, Louisiana, and Maine have already taken this step. The *New York Times* points out that Los Angeles and Chicago have done the same, and the whole state of California is considering it.

The Rationale for Smoking Bans

Let's step back and recall how we got here. When tobacco fighters began to outlaw smoking in elevators, buses, restaurants, bars, and public buildings, their stated rationale was to protect nonsmokers trapped inside. Then the crusade moved on to apartment buildings, extending the same theory: You can't smoke in your apartment, because the smoke seeps under your door into hallways and other people's apartments.

Now this rationale has moved outdoors. Way outdoors. David Kessler, the former FDA [U.S. Food and Drug Administration] commissioner who led the anti-smoking fight in the 1990s, says New York City is doing the right thing, because "the majority of the population today doesn't want to be breathing in tobacco smoke, whether indoors or outdoors."

That's true. I hate tobacco smoke. I don't want to breathe it anywhere. I don't want the tiniest particle of it to touch my lungs, even if my nose doesn't notice it.

But do I have the right to that standard of purity? If so, doesn't that justify a ban on smoking absolutely anywhere? Forget parks and beaches. If you smoke in your backyard, aren't you violating my airspace? In fact, aren't you violating my airspace by lighting your grill or driving your car down my street? How far does my right to clean air extend?

The Issue of Secondhand Smoke

Studies have proved that secondhand smoke is harmful. But those studies aren't conducted in wide-open spaces. They can't cover the whole atmosphere. They're conducted in enclosed spaces. That's why

The viewpoint's author believes that the outdoor ban on smoking instituted by Thomas Farley (left), New York City's Health Commissioner, goes too far.

they justify smoking bans in elevators and restaurants, not in acres and acres of parkland. New York's health commissioner, Thomas Farley, suggests that parks are defined spaces. Here's his argument, as quoted by the *Post*:

> "We don't think children, parents, when they're standing at soccer games, should have to be breathing in smoke from the person next to them," Farley said after unveiling the city's 10-point plan alongside Mayor Bloomberg. "We don't think our children should have to be watching someone smoke."

Whoa, there. First of all, you don't have to ban smoking on every square inch of park land in order to protect nonsmokers from "the person next to them." You can chalk off spaces where smoking is prohibited. Believe me, I coach kids' soccer games. Last week, some guys who work for the county league showed up to paint new lines on our practice field. If you can paint boundaries for play, you can paint boundaries for smoking. Want to keep smokers 100 yards away from where kids are playing? Draw a line.

Going Too Far

But check out Farley's second argument: Kids shouldn't "have to be watching someone smoke." We're no longer talking about breathing even a particle of smoke. We're talking about banning bad habits to prevent cultural contamination.

In that case, can we please ban public lotteries? Because I don't like my kids having to watch people gamble, particularly under the auspices of the state. Gambling is addictive and destructive. I want the tickets out of convenience stores and the results off television.

Why is a huge outdoor smoking ban justified even in the absence of substantiating medical evidence? Because, as one anti-smoking leader tells the *Times*, "There is no redeeming value in smoking at beaches

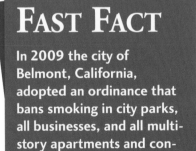

FAST FACT

In 2009 the city of Belmont, California, adopted an ordinance that bans smoking in city parks, all businesses, and all multi-story apartments and condominiums.

or parks." That's the bottom line: Any basis for a ban, no matter how slight, is now sufficient, because the value of smoking is zero.

Once we agree on that, the movement to ban smoking, having conquered the outdoors, can move back indoors, this time without any reference to other people's health. Because the value of smoking is zero in your bathroom, too.

EVALUATING THE AUTHORS' ARGUMENTS:

In this viewpoint Saletan claims that the right to clean air is not absolute. Are there any authors in this chapter who you think would disagree with this? Explain your answer.

Chapter 3

What Kind of Social Policies Should Be Used to Reduce Smoking?

Although social policies are in place to reduce smoking, their effectiveness may be questioned.

Antismoking Programs Work to Reduce Smoking

Michael Eriksen

"Counter-marketing campaigns . . . are effective in reducing smoking rates and the social acceptability of smoking."

In the following viewpoint, Michael Eriksen argues that campaigns aimed at preventing teen nicotine addiction work. Eriksen claims that one of the most effective ways to reduce smoking, especially among teens, is by creating counter-marketing campaigns that reveal the truth about tobacco use. He argues that the Truth Campaign has been particularly effective and should be continued. Eriksen is a professor and director of the Institute of Public Health at Georgia State University. He was director of the Office on Smoking and Health of the federal government's Centers for Disease Control and Prevention from 1992 to 2000.

Michael Eriksen, "Do Anti-Smoking Programs Work to Reduce Smoking? Yes: Programs Needed to Combat Billions Spent by Tobacco Companies," *Atlanta Journal-Constitution*, July 21, 2009, p. A11. Reproduced by permission of the author.

AS YOU READ, CONSIDER THE FOLLOWING QUESTIONS:
1. Eriksen claims that the decision to begin smoking is almost always made by teenagers who want what?
2. The author claims that the Truth Campaign reduced the risk of starting to smoke by what percent?
3. Eriksen argues that smoking is perpetuated by cigarette company marketing and can be extinguished by what?

Everyone knows that smoking kills, but few really appreciate the magnitude of the problem. Smoking is the leading cause of death in society, causing one out of every five deaths, and killing one out of two lifetime smokers.

Teen Nicotine Addiction

Even fewer people realize that beginning to smoke is almost always an adolescent decision made in response to teenagers wanting to appear cool, independent, sophisticated and glamorous—the aspirations of every teen and the very attributes promoted for decades by cigarette companies. It is no surprise that most adolescents that smoke show symptoms of nicotine addiction and want to quit smoking, but can't, even before graduating from high school.

The real tragedy is that we know how to prevent the problem of teen nicotine addiction, but fail to act. Rigorous scientific research has shown that price increases, strict advertising restrictions and clean indoor air laws are effective in reducing smoking for everyone, but are particularly effective among young people. The research evidence also shows that counter-marketing campaigns, particularly those aimed at debunking the carefully constructed myths of the tobacco industry that make smoking appear to be the cool thing to do, are effective in reducing smoking rates and the social acceptability of smoking.

The Truth Campaign

When I directed the CDC's [Centers for Disease Control and Prevention] Office on Smoking and Health, we wanted to learn how to use marketing techniques to keep kids from starting to smoke and convened an expert panel of teen marketing experts from the private sector.

Experts from companies like Adidas, Levi-Straus, and Proctor and Gamble—companies that sell products to teens—advised us that if we wanted to be successful in competing with the tobacco industry's multibillion-dollar effort to get people to smoke, we needed to do more than educate teens on the harm of smoking, and rather create a "brand" that would compete with the cigarette brands that appealed to young people, namely Marlboro (with its cowboy), Camel (with its Joe Camel campaign), and Newport (with its "Alive with Pleasure" campaign).

The experts recommended that the nonsmoking "brand" that might appeal most to youth was one that told the truth about smoking, i.e., that smoking really provided none of the attributes seen in the cigarette advertisements, but was in fact an expensive, dirty, smelly habit,

The "Truth Campaign" initiated by the American Legacy Foundation has helped to curb teen smoking. The campaign's focus is opening the eyes and minds of teens by revealing the truth about the dangers of smoking and exposing the lies they say tobacco companies perpetuate.

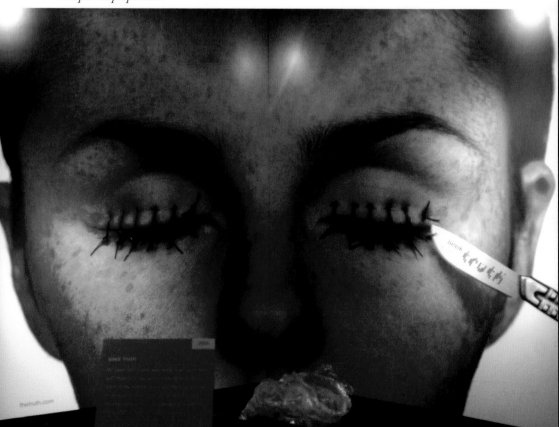

and that the cigarette companies were simply lying to them to increase their profits.

This "brand" became known as the "Truth Campaign" and was successfully used in Florida with funds from its settlement with the tobacco industry, and was rolled out nationally by the American Legacy Foundation as an outgrowth of the 1998 Master Settlement Agreement. The Truth Campaign was unprecedented in its success. Recent analysis found that exposure to the campaign reduced the risk of starting to smoke by 20 percent, resulting in 450,000 fewer adolescent smokers, and this was done in a cost-effective manner, with every $1 spent on the counter-marketing effort resulting in a savings of $6 of future medical costs averted.

FAST FACT

According to the Truth Campaign, cigarettes kill over 50 people an hour.

The campaign was so successful, in fact, that the Lorillard Tobacco Co. sued the Legacy Foundation to cease the campaign under the guise that the advertisements vilified them.

The Need for Counter-Marketing

Smoking is perpetuated by cigarette company marketing, and smoking can be extinguished by effective counter-marketing. But the counter-marketing has to be hard-hitting, sophisticated and appealing to adolescents and young adults showing them the "truth" about smoking and also graphically depicting how devastating smoking can be to those you care about or identify with.

The tobacco industry hates the truth and hates counter-marketing campaigns that tell the truth. Why? Because it works. Given the tobacco industry has recently been found guilty in a federal district court of racketeering and perpetuating a fraud on the American people, upheld in a May [2009] federal appeals court decision, it seems to be that there is a need for more "truth" and not less.

EVALUATING THE AUTHORS'
ARGUMENTS:

In this viewpoint Eriksen claims that the Truth Campaign has been successful in reducing smoking. What alternative explanation does Patrick Basham, author of the following viewpoint, give to explain the decline in the smoking rate?

Antismoking Programs Do Not Work to Reduce Smoking

Patrick Basham

> "Most tobacco control efforts have failed because they have not been linked to the right predictors of becoming a smoker."

In the following viewpoint, Patrick Basham argues that current tobacco control programs are not effective in fighting tobacco use. Basham claims that the states have misspent money received from the Master Settlement Agreement for smoking prevention and spent money on programs that do not work. Basham believes that raising standards of living is a far better way to prevent tobacco use than the prevention programs. Basham is founding director of the Democracy Institute and an adjunct scholar with the Cato Institute's Center for Representative Government.

Patrick Basham, "Up in Smoke," *Baltimore Sun*, July 28, 2008, p. A11. Reproduced by permission of the author.

AS YOU READ, CONSIDER THE FOLLOWING QUESTIONS:

1. According to Basham how much money did the Master Settlement Agreement give to states over 25 years?
2. What two smoking prevention programs does the author specifically discuss as having failed?
3. What erroneous assumption have antitobacco groups been operating under for the last 25 years, according to Basham?

Two recent events underscore big problems with the way society tries to fight tobacco use. First, a new Harvard study came out alleging that the tobacco industry manipulated menthol levels in cigarettes to hook young smokers in violation of the 1998 Master Settlement Agreement, which bans tobacco companies from targeting youths. And second, billionaires Michael R. Bloomberg and Bill Gates last week threw their support behind a new $500 million worldwide effort to stop smoking.

Whatever the tobacco companies may have done with menthol levels, the bigger scandal is how states have misspent the billions paid to them by the tobacco industry. And however well-intentioned, the Gates-Bloomberg effort, which involves the Johns Hopkins Bloomberg School of Public Health, is likely to fail because the tobacco control programs that it will fund—featuring such things as higher taxes, smoking bans and advertising restrictions—have failed before. These multiple shortcomings point to the need for a new, more effective approach to handling, and funding, tobacco prevention.

The Master Settlement Agreement

The Master Settlement Agreement resulted in a payment of $206 billion by the tobacco industry to 46 states over 25 years for smoking prevention. The states also receive annual payments in perpetuity based on inflation and cigarette sales.

When the agreement was signed, the state attorneys general pledged that this massive windfall would go toward funding smoking prevention programs. However, from the moment the states got their hands

The Sum of Master Settlement Agreement Payments, Through 2025

State	Settlement ($ in millions)	State	Settlement ($ in millions)
Alabama	3,166	New Hampshire	1,305
Alaska	669	New Jersey	7,576
Arizona	2,888	New Mexico	1,168
Arkansas	1,622	New York	25,003
California	25,007	North Carolina	4,569
Colorado	2,686	North Dakota	717
Connecticut	3,637	Ohio	9,869
Delaware	775	Oklahoma	2,030
DC	1,189	Oregon	2,248
Georgia	4,809	Pennsylvania	11,259
Hawaii	1,179	Rhode Island	1,408
Idaho	712	South Carolina	2,305
Illinois	9,119	South Dakota	684
Indiana	3,996	Tennessee	4,782
Iowa	1,704	Utah	872
Kansas	1,633	Vermont	806
Kentucky	3,450	Virginia	4,006
Louisiana	4,419	Washington	4,023
Maine	1,507	West Virginia	1,737
Maryland	4,429	Wisconsin	4,060
Massachusetts	7,913	Wyoming	487
Michigan	8,526	American Samoa	30
Missouri	4,456	Guam	43
Montana	832	N. Marianas	17
Nebraska	1,166	U.S. Virgin Islands	34
Nevada	1,195	Puerto Rico	2,197

Total = 195, 919 ($ in millions)

Note: These figures do not include the 4 states that settled individually with the tobacco companies (i.e., Florida, Minnesota, Mississippi, and Texas).

Taken from: CRS Report for Congress, "Tobacco Master Settlement Agreement (1998): Overview, Implementation by States, and Congressional Issues," November 5, 1999.

on the tobacco settlement money, this has not been the case. Instead of being spent on smoking prevention, the billions have gone to such things as expanded broadband cable networks, museum development, sewer upgrades, new schools and parks, economic development and general tax rebates.

Maryland's share of the settlement is $4.4 billion over 25 years. Yet the state falls short of the minimum amount recommended by the U.S. Centers for Disease Control and Prevention for state tobacco prevention spending: $30.3 million per year. According to the Campaign for Tobacco-Free Kids, in fiscal year 2007, Maryland spent only $18.7 million from tobacco settlement and tax revenues to prevent and reduce tobacco use.

The CDC recommends that the states invest 20 percent to 25 percent of the money they receive in tobacco control. Only three states (Maine, Delaware and Colorado) are funding their smoking prevention efforts at the CDC-recommended level. According to the Campaign for Tobacco-Free Kids, the states will receive $24.9 billion this year from the settlement and tobacco taxes, of which they will spend approximately 3 percent on tobacco control.

Dr. Asif Qadri, at the MCC Medical Clinic in Silver Springs, Maryland, urges his patient, who supports his family on his $7 per hour job at a gas station, to quit smoking. Reports indicate that socioeconomic state may be a factor in becoming a smoker.

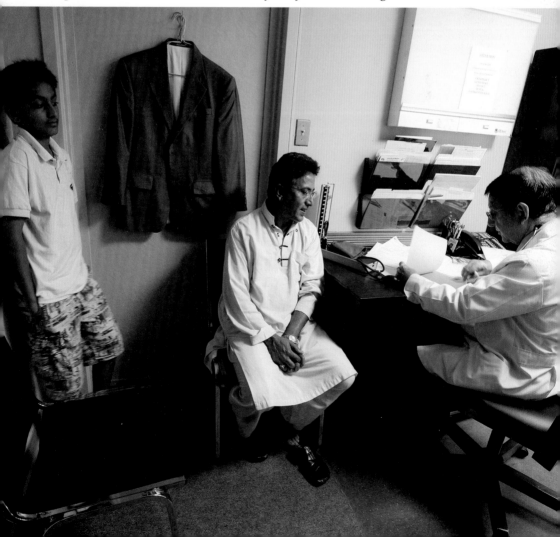

The Failed Efforts

Yet the tobacco settlement scandal is greater than the states' refusal to spend money for tobacco control on tobacco control. That's because even the meager efforts they do undertake bear little fruit.

For example, an enormous smoking prevention program in 11 communities called COMMIT (Community Intervention Trial for Smoking Cessation) was designed to help smokers, particularly heavy smokers, quit. It was a huge failure. Similarly, the largest attempt to put smoking prevention theory into practice was the American Stop Smoking Intervention Study (ASSIST), an eight-year project involving 17 states and run by the National Cancer Institute. This project possessed all of the bells and whistles of traditional smoking prevention: limiting tobacco advertising, restricting public smoking and making it harder for kids to access tobacco. Nevertheless, the project failed to produce a statistically significant reduction in smoking prevalence and consumption.

FAST FACT

The Initiative to Reduce Tobacco Use, or Bloomberg Initiative, supports tobacco control in China, India, Indonesia, the Russian Federation, and Bangladesh.

True, the U.S. smoking rate has declined sharply, but this trend began before the onset of significant government regulation and has continued, in large measure, because our society has continued to grow wealthier. Higher incomes stimulate public interest in, and concern about, matters of personal and public health.

The Right Predictors

A big part of the problem is that most anti-tobacco groups spent the last 25 years operating on the erroneous assumption that if you could prevent the tobacco industry from marketing, you could stop people from smoking. Most tobacco control efforts have failed because they have not been linked to the right predictors of becoming a smoker. These include socioeconomic status, connection and success at school, self-esteem, family structure and relations with parents.

Likewise, the $500 million in the Gates-Bloomberg plan would be far better spent on advocating for educational, economic and trade policies that would raise living standards and, consequently, dampen public interest in smoking—without the heavy hand of government intervention.

Ten years and $53 billion after the tobacco settlement windfall, there is precious little to show in terms of credible smoking prevention. It's time for Congress—and perhaps the president—to step in and demand that the states live up to their promise to use the settlement money for effective tobacco prevention. To ensure the settlement money has an impact, it needs to be diverted from projects unrelated to smoking and then placed into interventions that are based on what the best evidence shows are the real reasons kids start using cigarettes.

Until that happens, anti-tobacco efforts—whether funded by the states or by well-intentioned billionaires—will continue to amount to little more than blowing smoke.

EVALUATING THE AUTHORS' ARGUMENTS:

In this viewpoint Basham claims that tobacco prevention programs do not work but that raising standards of living does. What response do you think Michael Eriksen, author of the previous viewpoint, would have to this?

Raising Cigarette Taxes Is a Good Idea

Patrick Johnson

"Because the only gain of smoking a cigarette is a brief buzz or the continuation of an unhealthy addiction, smokers have to bear a financial burden."

In the following viewpoint Patrick Johnson contends that it is appropriate to single out cigarettes for tax increases. Johnson claims that because cigarettes are not necessary, it makes sense to tax them rather than essential items such as food. Johnson notes that many states and countries tax cigarettes heavily, and he claims that such taxes bring numerous economic benefits. Finally, Johnson concludes that a tax increase may have the benefit of causing smokers to quit. Johnson is a journalism student at the University of Wisconsin, Madison.

AS YOU READ, CONSIDER THE FOLLOWING QUESTIONS:
1. Johnson contends that the cigarette tax in Wisconsin rose to what in 2008?
2. According to the author, what is the tax on cigarettes in Greece?
3. The author claims that cigarettes sold in Wisconsin dropped by what percent in 2008?

Between working longer hours, paying more bills and getting fewer paychecks, some reach for a cigarette to take a break. But during an economic crisis where cigarettes may be needed the most, they're becoming more expensive due to federal and state tax increases, and rightfully so.

Cigarettes Are Not Necessary

Last year [2008] in Wisconsin, the tax on a pack of cigarettes swelled to a whopping $1.77, and Wisconsin has seen a great deal of success because of it. Gov. Jim Doyle has even expressed regret that he didn't push for 25 more cents when he could. However, it looks like Doyle will try to push that last 25 cent increase through with his budget proposal.

In a time of economic crisis, rather than taxing income more and taking money away from people who can use the money for necessities like food, taxing discretionary goods like cigarettes and alcohol is beneficial because it deters people from an unhealthy habit while still allowing smokers to enjoy their inconvenience to the state, though for a price.

Some may retort, "Why should smokers be singled out and punished because of the economic situation?"

Because the only gain of smoking a cigarette is a brief buzz or the continuation of an unhealthy addiction, smokers have to bear a financial burden to continue hedonistic habits. The same would apply for alcohol and other indulgent behaviors. To say this is not patronizing or lofty but realistic, because when economic crisis is affecting everyone in some way, sacrifices need to be made and cigarette smoking is simply one of the least necessary habits.

On April 1, 2009, the federal tax on packs of cigarettes rose from $0.37 to $1.01, the largest tobacco tax ever.

The Cigarette Tax in Other States

Comparatively, the possible cigarette tax increase would make Wisconsin one of the highest smoker-taxing states, weighing in at $1.77 per pack in taxes. The fifty states are fairly polarized with their taxing, so arguing that Wisconsin's tax is already too high isn't very conclusive or reassuring for those who think raising the tax is unfair.

As of January 2009, New York had the highest state cigarette tax with $2.75 per pack, while Midwestern states like Minnesota bear a $1.50 tax and Illinois's is just 98 cents.

The tax on alcohol, gas and income is the same way. Each state has duly created its own unique conception of what is allowed to be taxed and in what capacity. The tax of a gallon of spirits ranges from $2 dollars per gallon in one state to $20 dollars in another, making the further polarization of the cigarette tax something more reasonable.

The proposed cigarette tax increase, [which,] including the federal increase [would add up to taxes of] $3.02, would make an average pack of cigarettes in Wisconsin $5.02, with just over 60 percent of the retail price going to taxes.

Greece—the country with the worst smoking habit in the European Union—is increasing its cigarette tax from 75 to 80 percent and almost every member of the European Union has a higher tax on cigarettes by percentage of retail price than any state in our country. Taxing cigarettes heavily is not unusual and makes sense because smoking is something only narrowly beneficial and widely detrimental for personal health, fortune, and state prosperity.

The Economic Benefits

Taxing smokers has become a very successful economic move for many governments, including Wisconsin. Last year's tax increase brought a boon of $543.2 million to Wisconsin, according to a *Wisconsin State Journal* article. There are also indirect benefits of taxing cigarettes, like the vast health care costs directly tied with cigarette smoking that would be eliminated. A University of Michigan–Ann Arbor study attributes a conservative six to eight percent of health care costs as directly resulting from the smoking of cigarettes. According to anti-smoking campaigners, fewer

FAST FACT

As of November 2009, the cigarette tax in Wisconsin was up to $2.52 per pack, the sixth highest in the nation.

cigarettes means an estimated $480 million saved in smoking-related health care costs because each smoker accrues something like 5,000 dollars in medical costs each year.

This is a ton of money, enough to solve a lot of problems for the state. Some people may see health care costs resulting from smoking as a huge profit for the health care industry—one of the nation's greatest —making widespread cigarette smoking a source of profit. However, it would be insensitive for the state to be dissuaded from providing a disincentive to smoking, keeping us sick, to keep the health care industry thriving.

Dissuading Smokers

A *Wisconsin State Journal* article reports that advocates of the bill esti-mate that the proposed tax increase will help 10 percent of smokers quit smoking. Last year the number of cigarettes sold in Wisconsin dropped by almost 18 percent, according to the Legislature's budget office.

If increasing the price of cigarettes means that less people are getting their fix, that's okay. Cigarettes have such negligible benefits for the smoker in comparison to the detriments they create for the people

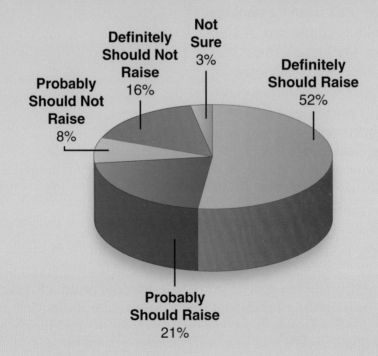

Raising Cigarette Taxes

In a 2007 Harris poll, the following question was asked:

"If taxes had to be raised in order to increase revenues, how would you feel about raising the following types of federal taxes"

This chart reflects the responses concerning cigarette taxes.

Definitely Should Not Raise 16%

Not Sure 3%

Definitely Should Raise 52%

Probably Should Not Raise 8%

Probably Should Raise 21%

around them and the state, let alone for themselves. If smokers feel that a tax increase is unfair, they have to work a little harder to pay for their fix and realize their indulgence is self-serving when people should have to help serve each other.

EVALUATING THE AUTHORS' ARGUMENTS:

In this viewpoint Johnson claims that it is fair to single out cigarette smokers for tax increases. What is his reasoning? Would Patrick Fleenor, author of the following viewpoint, agree or disagree?

Raising Cigarette Taxes Is Not a Good Idea

Patrick Fleenor

> "*Hiking what is already one of the most unfair and disruptive taxes on the books will only increase the harm to smokers and nonsmokers alike.*"

In the following viewpoint Patrick Fleenor argues that it would be unfair to further tax cigarettes. Fleenor rejects the view that because smoking is risky, higher taxes are justified. Rather, Fleenor contends that smokers are already taxed more than their fair share to compensate for any economic burden on society. Further taxes, he argues, would simply increase the illegal trade of cigarettes, resulting in lawlessness that affects everyone negatively. Fleenor is chief economist at the Tax Foundation, an organization that educates taxpayers about sound tax policy and the size of the tax burden borne by Americans at all levels of government.

AS YOU READ, CONSIDER THE FOLLOWING QUESTIONS:
1. Fleenor compares smoking to what other two risky activities?
2. What is the externality, or cost imposed on society, for every pack of cigarettes smoked, according to Fleenor?
3. According to the author, how much can bootleggers earn on each truckload of cigarettes smuggled into California currently?

Nicholas Goldberg's "How and why taxes go up, in smoke" [in the *Los Angeles Times*, June 14, 2009] reads more like a press release from the anti-smoking lobby than an objective question-and-answer backgrounder: Smoking is bad and the state needs more money, therefore hiking the cigarette tax is good. If smokers quit, so much the better. It's a win-win!

Oh, if life were only so simple.

A Society of Different Values

An overarching theme of the article is that smoking is simply a bad thing. Yet we live in a diverse society in which tastes vary widely. For some, total bliss is a pack of Marlboros and a day at the monster truck show; for others, it's a bottle of Cabernet and a night at the opera. There is no reason one group should be subject to punitive taxes while the other is praised for its sophistication.

The fact that something is risky doesn't make it bad. Some people ride motorcycles and sunbathe; like smoking, these are risky activities. Are they therefore bad? No. As long as people understand the risks of

FAST FACT

On April 1, 2009, the federal tax on cigarettes increased by 62 cents, to $1.01 per pack.

what they are doing and bear all of the costs, there is no reason for the government to threaten to impoverish them if they don't live their lives in the way some bureaucrat demands.

Life in a free society requires tolerance of activities that have little or no effect on others, even those we don't personally approve of. If

Steve-O of the film Jackass *is a famous risk-taker. The author of this viewpoint argues that risk-takers, such as smokers and others, should not be punished because their tastes differ from others, as long as they bear the costs of their risk-taking.*

government or interest groups have information about risks that are not widely known, they should disseminate it. Otherwise, adults should be left alone to live their lives in accordance with their own dreams and values.

The Tyranny of the Majority

Goldberg also points out that "smoking is unpopular, and smokers are politically weak," so why not raise tobacco taxes? Is tyranny of the majority, the classic danger of democracy that Alexis de Tocqueville warned about, really something Californians want to embrace? Of course not. Instead, we should ask, what is an equitable division of the tax burden? Presumably we all benefit from government services. Then we should all pay for them.

A special tax on cigarettes could be justified if smokers were foisting some costs onto their fellow citizens. This subject has been studied extensively by some of the nation's leading economists, who have found that there is indeed a small "externality" associated with smoking —about 35 cents per pack. However, because federal and state cigarette taxes are far in excess of this amount, the current fiscal system transfers billions of dollars from relatively low-income smokers to higher-income nonsmokers. If anything, tax fairness calls for a reduction of the cigarette tax, certainly not a higher one.

The Risk of Lawlessness
Goldberg spends much of his time discussing how the law of demand —the common-sense idea that as the price of something rises the quantity demanded by consumers falls—can be used to snuff out

"Smokers," cartoon by Ed Fischer, www.CartoonStock.com. Copyright © Ed Fischer. Reproduction rights obtainable from www.CartoonStock.com.

smoking. Unfortunately, he glosses over another economic concept, the notion of a substitute good—in this case, bootleg cigarettes—that undermines his argument.

Right now, it is possible for bootleggers to earn more than $400,000 on every truckload of cigarettes smuggled into the Golden State. Those from a foreign source can fetch five times that amount. These illicit profits are the reason the California Board of Equalization estimates that the state loses more than $275 million annually to tobacco tax evasion.

It doesn't take a Nobel laureate to know what would happen if the cigarette tax were doubled or tripled. The marked rise in bootlegging would mitigate any health benefits of the hike. Moreover, as commerce migrates from the corner store to the street corner, youth access to tobacco products would probably increase.

A higher tax would also probably trigger a wave of cigarette thefts, a problem that has plagued the state in the wake of past tax hikes. The increase in such lawlessness coupled with the rise in the crimes traditionally associated with black markets—murders from deals gone bad, gun battles over turf and so on—would adversely affect smokers and nonsmokers alike.

There are no easy answers to California's budget woes. These problems have been building for decades. Perhaps it's time for citizens to fundamentally reappraise exactly what they want the state government to do and devise a fair and efficient tax system for collecting revenue. Hiking what is already one of the most unfair and disruptive taxes on the books will only increase the harm to smokers and nonsmokers alike.

EVALUATING THE AUTHOR'S ARGUMENTS:

In this viewpoint Fleenor makes several points to support his argument. Which point do you find most convincing? Why?

Eliminating Smoking in Movies Will Help Reduce Teen Smoking

Ralph Nader

"It is so important to get smoking out of kid-rated films."

In the following viewpoint Ralph Nader argues that smoking needs to be eliminated from kid-rated films. Nader claims that although much progress has been made socially against cigarettes, smoking in movies is still commonplace. Nader argues that smoking in movies that children see makes them more likely to take up smoking. The cure, Nader claims, is to give R-ratings to movies that feature cigarette smoking, a change the industry has resisted. Nader is an attorney, consumer advocate, author, and four-time presidential candidate.

Ralph Nader, "Making Cancer Cool: Tobacco and Hollywood," *CounterPunch*, February 17, 2007. Copyright © 2008 Counterpunch, LLP. Reproduced by permission.

AS YOU READ, CONSIDER THE FOLLOWING QUESTIONS:
1. According to Nader, what percent of U.S. movie releases have smoking scenes?
2. What percent of people expected to die from smoking-related diseases by 2025 will be in developing countries, according to Nader?
3. During the lead-up to awards shows, did public health groups and agencies demand that Hollywood end its relationship with Big Tobacco, according to the author?

A mong the greatest unsung public health advances of recent times is progress made against the global cigarette industry.

Progress Against Cigarettes

In the United States, cigarette smoking is finally on the decline. The courts have ruled the tobacco industry to be "racketeers." Smokefree spaces, including not just workplaces but restaurants and bars, are proliferating, reducing the harms of second-hand smoke and encouraging millions to quit. States are raising cigarette taxes, reducing smoking and raising funds for important public health programs.

Internationally, progress is speeding even faster. A global treaty, the Framework Convention on Tobacco Control, is encouraging countries to adopt far-reaching anti-smoking measures, including bans on all cigarette advertisements. Countries are emulating and surpassing the smokefree initiatives in the United States—even Irish pubs are now smokefree!

But despite all the public health gains, Big Tobacco is still on the move, addicting millions more smokers. And the industry has some unfortunate allies.

Smoking in Movies

One important cultural ally of Big Tobacco is Hollywood. Smoking in youth-rated movies is on the rise, and it has demonstrable effects on smoking rates.

According to researchers at the University of California San Francisco Center for Tobacco Control Research and Education, smoking appears even more in Hollywood movies released with G/PG/PG-13 than in R-rated films. Altogether, 75 percent of all U.S. releases have smoking scenes. One cartoon film now on DVD, *The Ant Bully*, includes 41 tobacco scenes.

Researchers have found that viewing smoking in movies makes it far more likely that children will take up the habit—controlling for all other relevant factors (such as whether parents and peers smoke).

Think about it—the movies are glamorous, and they portray smoking as glamorous, whether or not it is a good guy or bad guy lighting a cigarette.

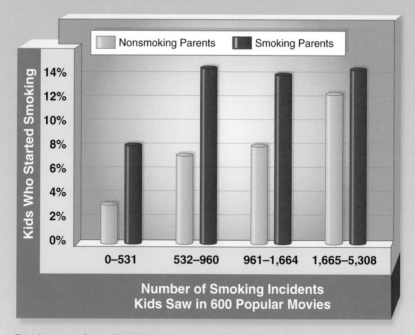

Effect of Smoking in Movies on Adolescent Smoking Rates

The more smoking adolescents see in movies, the more likely they are to start smoking. The effect is most dramatic for children of nonsmokers.

Taken from: James Sargent, Smoke Free Movies: www.smokefreemovies.ucsf.edu
[http://www.smokefreemovies.ucsf.edu/godeeper/Landmark_Study.html].

The public health advances against Big Tobacco are due in significant part to effective efforts to vilify the industry. When children especially appreciate how the companies are manipulating them, they resist. Hollywood's glorification of smoking works directly against this.

U.S. films bring in 30 percent of movie box office sales globally, and Hollywood's contribution to smoking is significant overseas, where the tobacco epidemic is worst. Ten million people are expected to die every year from smoking-related disease by 2025, 70 percent of them in developing countries. Hollywood movies have gigantic appeal overseas, often with even greater cultural influence than in the United States. They appeal exactly to the demographic most likely to take up smoking—urbanized, middle-class youth who aspire to Western lifestyles.

An Easy Cure

This is an easy problem to cure. Leading U.S. health groups and the United Nation's World Health Organization have urged Hollywood to adopt R-ratings for movies with tobacco scenes (with exceptions where the presentation of tobacco clearly and unambiguously reflects the dangers and consequences of tobacco use or is necessary to represent the smoking of a real historical figure), to air anti-tobacco spots before films with tobacco imagery, to certify that movies with tobacco received no tobacco industry payoffs, and to stop identifying tobacco brands in movies. None of these measures involves any "censorship."

The industry has resisted.

This week [February 19–25, 2007] leading up to the 79th Annual Academy Awards, public health groups and agencies from New York and Los Angeles, from Liverpool and Sydney have mobilized to demand that Hollywood end its complicity with Big Tobacco.

In Washington, DC, representatives of the Smokefree Movies Action Network, dressed in biohazard suits, called on the Motion Picture

Protesters in Washington DC in July 2006 call on Hollywood to stop glorifying smoking in movies. A large poster of the film The Stepford Wives *has been installed with a warning sign that reads "This Movie Contains Tobacco Use. May Leave Youthful Audiences Three Times More Likely to Smoke."*

Association of America [MPAA] to remove "toxic" tobacco content from youth rated films. They presented the MPAA with a "golden coffin."

The trade association's representatives declined to accept the award.

The celebration of film at the Oscars reminds us of Hollywood's reach. That's exactly why it is so important to get smoking out of kid-rated films.

EVALUATING THE AUTHOR'S ARGUMENTS:

In this viewpoint Nader relates the changes that U.S. health groups and the World Health Organization have suggested the U.S. movie industry adopt. Do you feel that these changes would have an impact on teens watching movies? Do you agree with Nader that these changes do not amount to censorship?

There Is No Evidence That Smoking in Movies Causes Kids to Start Smoking

Jacob Sullum

"The weakest link in the chain of reasoning . . . is the assumption that half of the teenagers who start smoking do so because they saw it in the movies."

In the following viewpoint Jacob Sullum argues that concerns about smoking in movies are unfounded. He claims that smoking in movies is no more common than smoking in life. He also criticizes the evidence put forward for the view that smoking in movies causes kids to smoke, claiming that the studies testing this theory were flawed. He rejects the proposal to give movies with smoking an R rating and suggests that the real causes of smoking are found elsewhere—not in the movies. Sullum is a senior editor at *Reason* magazine and Reason.com, and is also a nationally syndicated columnist.

I n the 2005 movie *The Jacket*, Kelly Lynch plays a drunk who burns to death after falling asleep while smoking. According to the activists who object to cinematic smoking, Lynch's character is part of an insidious plot to lure children into the habit by making it seem cool and glamorous.

The movie research cited by anti-smoking activists typically defines pro-tobacco messages broadly enough to include all instances of smoking, actual or implied, along with discussions of tobacco and glimpses of cigarette logos, lighters, or ashtrays. A new study takes a more discriminating approach, looking at the behavior and characteristics of the leading characters in 447 popular films released since 1990, and comes to some rather different conclusions.

Smoking in Movies

Anti-smoking activists assert that smoking is more common in movies than it is in real life. The new study, reported in the August issue of the medical journal *Chest*, found that, overall, "contemporary American movies do not have a higher prevalence of smoking than the general U.S. population." The activists complain that movies put cigarettes in the hands of attractive protagonists and link smoking to success and affluence. The *Chest* study found that "bad guys" were more likely to smoke than "good guys" and that, as in real life, smoking was associated with lower socioeconomic status.

"Most investigators have concluded that smoking is portrayed as glamorous and positive, but our study shows that the exact opposite is true," says lead author Karan Omidvari, a physician at St. Michael's

Medical Center in Newark. Likewise, there was no evidence to support the idea that movie studios conspire with tobacco companies to target women or minorities.

Having shown that the indictment of Hollywood for pushing cigarettes is based largely on weak studies and loose talk, Omidvari and his colleagues were quick to add that they nevertheless object to smoking in movies. According to Robert McCaffree, president of the foundation that publishes *Chest*, the study "emphasizes the need for change in this area, including increasing anti-tobacco messages in coming attractions and films."

Stanton Glantz of the Smoke Free Movies Organization displays his findings in 2004 of a five-year analysis of smoking in movies in Hollywood. This author believes that Glantz' theories were debunked by Karan Omidvari, a physician at St. Michael's Medical Center in Newark.

The Effect of Movie Smoking

Stanton Glantz, an anti-smoking activist who was involved in much of the research debunked by Omidvari's study, has a different solution in mind: a mandatory R rating for movies that include smoking. Last fall his Smoke Free Movies campaign took out full-page ads in *The New York Times* and other publications claiming that adopting this policy "would cut movie smoking's effect on kids in half, saving 50,000 lives a year in the U.S. alone."

It's hard to say how many teenagers would be deterred by greater use of the R rating—especially if their parents knew that a single smoking scene was enough to qualify an otherwise unobjectionable movie for the not-without-a-parent-or-guardian category. But the weakest

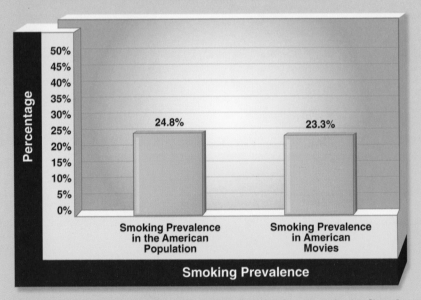

Smoking in Movies and Life

The article "Smoking in Contemporary American Cinema," published in the medical journal *Chest*, found that the prevalence of smoking in contemporary American movies is lower than the prevalence of smoking in the U.S. population.

Taken from: Karan Omidvari, Klaus Lessnau, Jeannie Kim, et al., "Smoking in Contemporary American Cinema," August 2005 [http://chestjournal.chestpubs.org/content/128/2/746.abstract].

link in the chain of reasoning that charges the Motion Picture Association of America with killing 137 (middle-aged or elderly) "kids" a day by failing to make this simple change in its rating system is the assumption that half of the teenagers who start smoking do so because they saw it in the movies.

That assumption is based on a 2003 *Lancet* study that found 10-to-14-year-olds who had seen movies with many smoking scenes were more likely to try cigarettes than kids who had seen movies with fewer smoking scenes. The problem with attributing this association to the modeling effect of cinematic smoking is that it's impossible to control for all the differences in personality and environment that make kids more likely to see movies with a lot of smoking in them, which already tend to be R-rated movies.

An Inconceivable Claim

Methodological difficulties aside, the size of this alleged effect is implausibly large, to put it mildly. In a commentary on the *Lancet* study, Glantz said cinematic smoking accounts for even more real-life smoking than advertising does: 52 percent vs. 34 percent. (He explained that is "probably because . . . the subliminal effects of smoking in movies is [sic] a more powerful force than overt advertising.") Is it even conceivable that exposure to movies and advertising causes 86 percent of smoking? That all other factors in life together contribute only 14 percent?

While such claims are patently absurd, there's an unstated premise that's even more offensive: that every filmmaker should make his work conform to the dictates of the health nannies. Omidvari and his colleagues found that smoking was especially common in independent films, a fact they said may be due to the "antiestablishment or free-spirited" character of such movies. If anyone is making smoking seem cool, it's self-righteous busybodies like Stanton Glantz.

> **FAST FACT**
>
> A 2005 study found that characters who smoke in movies are more likely to be male; white; the antagonist, or bad character; and from a lower socioeconomic class.

EVALUATING THE AUTHOR'S ARGUMENTS:

In this viewpoint Sullum asserts that a study claiming that smoking in movies caused kids to start smoking was flawed. Given his criticism, is a definitive study even possible? Explain your answer.

Facts About Smoking

Editor's note: These facts can be used in reports or papers to reinforce or add credibility when making important points or claims.

Health Effects of Cigarette Smoking
According to the Centers for Disease Control and Prevention (CDC):
- Smoking causes 90 percent of all lung cancer deaths in men.
- Smoking causes 80 percent of all lung cancer deaths in women.
- Smoking increases the risk of coronary heart disease by 2 to 4 times.
- Smoking increases the risk of stroke by 2 to 4 times.
- Smoking increases the risk of developing lung cancer by 13 times.
- Smoking harms nearly every organ of the body.

According to a 2008 survey by Rasmussen Reports:
- Eighty-seven percent of U.S. voters say people who smoke cigarettes today are generally aware of the health dangers, with 89 percent of current and former smokers compared with 86 percent of people who have never smoked saying they are aware.
- Seventy-one percent of U.S. voters say tobacco companies should not be held liable, or responsible, for health problems that smokers develop; 22 percent say the companies should be liable; the rest are undecided.

Secondhand Smoke
Facts About Secondhand Smoke
- Secondhand smoke is smoke from a burning cigarette, cigar, or pipe tip, or smoke exhaled by a person smoking a cigarette, cigar, or pipe.
- Secondhand smoke is also known as environmental tobacco smoke.

According to the Centers for Disease Control and Prevention (CDC):
- Secondhand smoke contains at least 250 toxic chemicals, including more than 50 that cause cancer.
- In children, secondhand smoke causes ear infections, more frequent and severe asthma attacks, respiratory symptoms and infections, and a greater risk for sudden infant death syndrome (SIDS).

- In adults who have never smoked, secondhand smoke at home or work increases the risk of heart disease by 25 to 30 percent.
- Exposure to secondhand smoke can increase the risk for heart attack.
- In adults who have never smoked, secondhand smoke at home or work increases the risk of lung cancer by 20 to 30 percent.
- Secondhand smoke exposure tends to be higher for African Americans, low-income persons, and blue-collar workers.

Laws Against Smoking

Existing Laws Against Smoking
- As of May 2010, there is no nationwide federal smoking ban; smoking bans are a result of state and local laws.
- As of May 2010, 26 states had statewide smoking bans in public enclosed areas with very few exemptions, 13 states had statewide bans with more permissible exemptions on certain establishments such as bars, and 11 states have no general statewide ban.

According to a 2008 survey by Rasmussen Reports:
- About one out of five U.S. voters (22 percent) say that the federal government should outlaw smoking.
- Nearly one-third of voters (32 percent) under the age of thirty believe smoking should be against the law.
- Fourteen percent of smokers, 22 percent of former smokers, and 23 percent of those who have never smoked think smoking should be against the law.

According to a 2007 Gallup poll:
- Approximately two out of every five Americans think smoking in all public places should be illegal.
- More than half of Americans favor a complete smoking ban in restaurants, whereas less than half want a complete smoking ban in workplaces, hotels, and bars.
- Fifty-one percent of smokers say that public smoking restrictions are justified; 47 percent of smokers say the increased restrictions make them feel unjustly discriminated against as a smoker.

Cigarette Taxes

State and Federal Cigarette Taxes
- As of May 2010, the federal tax on cigarettes is $1.01 per pack.
- Overall, the average state tax on cigarettes is $1.40 per pack.

- As of May 2010, Rhode Island had the highest state cigarette tax, at $3.46 per pack, whereas South Carolina had the lowest state cigarette tax, at 7¢ per pack.

According to a 2009 survey of smokers by Richard Day Research:
- Seventy percent of smokers say the price of cigarettes is one of their main concerns about smoking.
- Seventy-two percent of smokers said the April 2009 federal cigarette tax increase of 62¢ would make them more likely to quit smoking.

According to a 2009 survey of U.S. voters by Rasmussen Reports:
- American voters are evenly split on the issue of whether or not cigarette taxes discriminate against smokers, with 46 percent on each side and 8 percent undecided.
- Fifty-one percent of Republicans and 40 percent of Democrats think the so-called sin tax on cigarettes is a form of discrimination.
- Fifty-one percent of men but only 40 percent of women think the tax on cigarettes is discriminatory.

Organizations to Contact

The editors have compiled the following list of organizations concerned with the issues debated in this book. The descriptions are derived from materials provided by the organizations. All have publications or information available for interested readers. The list was compiled on the date of publication of the present volume; the information provided here may change. Be aware that many organizations take several weeks or longer to respond to inquiries, so allow as much time as possible for the receipt of requested materials.

Action on Smoking and Health (ASH)
2013 H St. NW, Washington, DC 20006
(202) 659-4310
Web site: www.ash.org

ASH is a national nonprofit legal action and educational organization fighting for the rights of nonsmokers against the many problems of smoking. ASH has worked to eliminate tobacco ads from radio and television and to ban smoking in airplanes, buses, and many public places. The organization publishes the bimonthly newsletter *The Smoking and Health Review* and fact sheets on a variety of topics, including teen smoking, passive smoking, and nicotine addiction.

American Cancer Society (ACS)
1599 Clifton Rd. NE, Atlanta, GA 30329
(800) ACS-2345 (227-2345)
Web site: www.cancer.org

ACS is a nationwide, community-based voluntary health organization. ACS spends a great deal of its resources on educating the public about the dangers of smoking and on lobbying for antismoking legislation. ACS makes available hundreds of publications, ranging from reports and surveys to position papers, including "Smoking in the Workplace."

American Council on Science and Health (ACSH)
1995 Broadway, 2nd Floor, New York, NY 10023-5860
(212) 362-7044
fax: (212) 362-4919
e-mail: acsh@acsh.org
Web site: www.acsh.org

ACSH is a consumer education group concerned with issues related to food, nutrition, chemicals, pharmaceuticals, lifestyle, the environment, and health. ACSH works to add reason and balance to debates about public health issues, such as tobacco use. It publishes the quarterly newsletter *Priorities* as well as position statements, including "Health Effects of Menthol in Cigarettes."

American Legacy Foundation
2030 M St. NW, 6th Floor, Washington, DC 20036
(202) 454-5555
fax: (202) 454-5999
e-mail: info@americanlegacy.org
Web site: www.americanlegacy.org

The American Legacy Foundation is dedicated to building a world where young people reject tobacco and anyone can quit using tobacco. The foundation works on the Truth campaign, a national tobacco youth prevention and education effort. It conducts extensive research on tobacco-related issues and publishes the results in *First Look Reports*, a series of brief summaries of its research.

American Lung Association
1740 Broadway, New York, NY 10019-4374
(212) 315-8700
fax: (212) 265-5642
e-mail: info@lungusa.org
Web site: www.lungusa.org

The American Lung Association is an organization working to save lives by improving lung health and preventing lung disease. Through education, advocacy, and research, the American Lung Association fights for healthy lungs and healthy air. The organization publishes an annual report, *State of Tobacco Control*, among other reports available at its Web site.

Americans for Nonsmokers' Rights (ANR)

2530 San Pablo Ave., Suite J, Berkeley, CA 94702
(510) 841-3032
fax: (510) 841-3071
e-mail: anr@no-smoke.org
Web site: www.no-smoke.org

ANR is a national lobbying organization dedicated to nonsmokers' rights. ANR pursues an action-oriented program of policy and legislation taking on the tobacco industry at all levels of government, protecting nonsmokers from exposure to secondhand smoke, and preventing tobacco addiction among youth. The organization publishes the quarterly newsletter *UPDATE*, in addition to maps of smoke-free laws, both available at its Web site.

Campaign for Tobacco-Free Kids

1400 Eye St. NW, Suite 1200, Washington, DC 20005
(202) 296-5469
fax: (202) 296-5427
Web site: www.tobaccofreekids.org

The Campaign for Tobacco-Free Kids is a nonprofit organization that works to reduce tobacco use. The Campaign for Tobacco-Free Kids fights to prevent kids from smoking, help smokers quit, and protect everyone from secondhand smoke. Available at the campaign's Web site are fact sheets and reports, including "Big Tobacco Targets Women and Girls."

Canadian Council for Tobacco Control (CCTC)

192 Bank St., Ottawa, ON K2P 1W8 Canada
(800) 267-5234
(613) 567-3050
fax: (613) 567-5695
e-mail: infoservices@cctc.ca
Web site: www.cctc.ca

The CCTC is a nongovernmental organization that works to promote a society free from tobacco addiction and involuntary exposure to tobacco products. It promotes a comprehensive tobacco control program involving educational, social, fiscal, and legislative interventions. It publishes several fact sheets, including "Youth and Tobacco" and "Secondhand Smoke: Health Effects."

Cato Institute
1000 Massachusetts Ave. NW, Washington, DC 20001-5403
(202) 842-0200
fax: (202) 842-3490
Web site: www.cato.org

The Cato Institute is a public policy research foundation dedicated to limiting the role of government, protecting individual liberties, and promoting free markets. The Cato Institute commissions a variety of publications, including books, monographs, briefing papers, and other studies. Among its publications are the quarterly magazine *Regulation* and the bimonthly *Cato Policy Report*, and a chapter from the *Cato Handbook for Policymakers*, "Tobacco and the Rule of Law."

Competitive Enterprise Institute (CEI)
1899 L St. NW, 12th Floor, Washington, DC 20036
(202) 331-1010
fax: (202) 331-0640
e-mail: info@cei.org
Web site: www.cei.org

CEI is a public interest group dedicated to free enterprise and limited government. CEI questions the validity and accuracy of Environmental Protection Agency studies that report the dangers of secondhand smoke. Its publications include policy studies and several newsletters, including *CEI Planet*, in which the recent article "Congress, Tobacco, and a President Who Lights Up," appeared.

FORCES International
PO Box 533, Sutton, WV 26601
(304) 765-5394
e-mail: info@forces.org
Web site: www.forces.org

FORCES International is an organization in support of human rights and the defense of the freedom to smoke, eat, drink, and, in general, enjoy personal lifestyle choices without restrictions and state interference.

FORCES fights against smoking ordinances and restrictions designed to eventually eliminate smoking, and it works to increase public awareness of smoking-related legislation. Its Web site includes articles about smoking and information about the health effects of smoking, including "Less Hazardous Cigarettes."

Foundation for Economic Education (FEE)
30 S. Broadway, Irvington-on-Hudson, NY 10533
(914) 591-7230
fax: (914) 591-8910
Web site: www.fee.org

FEE is a free-market organization. FEE promotes private property rights, the free market economic system, and limited government. FEE publishes a monthly journal, *The Freeman: Ideas on Liberty*, which has included many articles opposing regulation of the tobacco industry and opposing smoking bans.

National Institute on Drugs Abuse (NIDA)
6001 Executive Blvd., Room 5213, Bethesda, MD 20892-9561
(301) 443-6245
e-mail: information@nida.nih.gov
Web site: www.drugabuse.gov

NIDA is part of the National Institutes of Health (NIH), a component of the U.S. Department of Health and Human Services. NIDA supports and conducts research on drug abuse—including the yearly *Monitoring the Future Survey*—to improve addiction prevention, treatment, and policy efforts. It publishes the bimonthly *NIDA Notes* newsletter, the periodic *NIDA Capsules* fact sheets, and a catalog of research reports and public education materials, including the research report, "Tobacco Addiction."

Reason Foundation
3415 S. Sepulveda Blvd., Suite 400, Los Angeles, CA 90034
(310) 391-2245
fax: (310) 391-4395
Web site: www.reason.org

The Reason Foundation is a nonprofit organization advocating free markets and free minds. The Reason Foundation promotes choice, competition, and a dynamic market economy as the foundation for human dignity and progress. It has published many articles supporting smokers' rights and arguing against the so-called nanny state in the monthly magazine *Reason* and on its Web site, Reason.com.

U.S. Environmental Protection Agency (EPA)

Ariel Rios Bldg., 1200 Pennsylvania Ave. NW, Washington, DC 20460
(202) 272-0167
Web site: www.epa.gov

The EPA is the agency of the U.S. government that coordinates actions designed to protect human health and to safeguard the natural environment. The EPA's Smoke-Free Homes and Cars Program promotes indoor air free from environmental tobacco smoke. The EPA publishes numerous fact sheets and brochures, including "Secondhand Tobacco Smoke and the Health of Your Family."

For Further Reading

Books

Brandt, Allan M. *The Cigarette Century: The Rise, Fall, and Deadly Persistence of the Product That Defined America.* New York: Basic Books, 2009. Traces the remarkable rise and dramatic decline of cigarette consumption in the United States.

Burns, Eric. *The Smoke of the Gods: A Social History of Tobacco.* Philadelphia, PA: Temple University Press, 2007. Recounts the social history of tobacco, especially in the United States, arguing that it changed the course of history.

Califano, Joseph A., Jr. *High Society: How Substance Abuse Ravages America and What to Do About It.* New York: PublicAffairs, 2007. Argues that substance abuse is a critical problem in America and calls for further action to prevent youth from smoking, drinking alcohol, and using drugs.

Chapman, Simon. *Public Health Advocacy and Tobacco Control: Making Smoking History.* Malden, MA: Wiley-Blackwell, 2007. Lays out a program for eliminating smoking, critiquing ineffective approaches and providing strategies for making smoking obsolete.

Douglass, William Campbell. *The Health Benefits of Tobacco.* Miami, FL: Rhino, 2004. Contends that the benefits of smoking to mental and physical health outweigh the risks.

Fitzgerald, James. *The Joys of Smoking Cigarettes.* New York: Harper-Entertainment, 2007. Celebrates the pleasures of smoking with facts, trivia, classic advertisements, smoking celebrity photographs, and observations.

Gately, Iain. *Tobacco: A Cultural History of How an Exotic Plant Seduced Civilization.* New York: Grove, 2003. Contends that the tobacco trade was the driving force behind several key historical events, including the growth of the American colonies and victory in the American Revolution.

Goel, Rajeev K., and Michael A. Nelson. *Global Efforts to Combat Smoking.* Burlington, VT: Ashgate, 2008. Brings together the findings of economists on policy initiatives to combat smoking and draws conclusions regarding the efficacy of the various policy measures.

Hyde, Margaret O., and John F. Setaro. *Smoking 101: An Overview for Teens*. Minneapolis, MN: Twenty-First Century, 2006. Contains information on how smoking and secondhand smoke affect the human body, the debate over the right to smoke, and the status of lawsuits against tobacco companies.

Kuhn, Cynthia, Scott Swartzwelder, and Wilkie Wilson. *Buzzed: The Straight Facts About the Most Used and Abused Drugs from Alcohol to Ecstasy*. 3rd ed. New York: W.W. Norton, 2008. Relays information for understanding how drugs—such as nicotine—work and their effects on the body and behavior.

Libal, Joyce. *Putting Out the Fire: Smoking and the Law*. Broomall, PA: Mason Crest, 2009. Tells the story of the many attempts to regulate the tobacco industry, including those that failed and those that succeeded.

Michaels, David. *Doubt Is Their Product: How Industry's Assault on Science Threatens Your Health*. New York: Oxford University Press, 2008. Argues that the tobacco industry's deceitful tactics spawned a multimillion-dollar industry that is dismantling public health safeguards.

Pampel, Fred C. *Tobacco Industry and Smoking*. Rev. ed. New York: Facts On File, 2009. Addresses serious and controversial questions that pertain to smoking in the United States, with legal and historical overviews, reference resources, statistics, and a research guide.

Rabinoff, Michael. *Ending the Tobacco Holocaust*. Santa Rosa, CA: Elite Books, 2006. Contends that allowing tobacco companies to continue to do business as usual has enormous health and financial consequences.

Shafey, Omar, Michael Eriksen, Hana Ross, and Judith Mackay. *The Tobacco Atlas*. 3rd ed. Atlanta, GA: American Cancer Society, 2009. Illustrates a wide range of international tobacco issues through maps and graphs and predicts the future course of the tobacco epidemic globally.

Periodicals

Bast, Joseph. "Still Pooping in My Salad," *Heartlander*, April/May 2008.

Beato, Greg. "Politically Correct Political Incorrectness," *Globe & Mail*, November 9, 2009.

Blackwell, Ken. "First My Tobacco, Next My Guns," *Washington Times*, November 3, 2008.

Calfee, John E. "A Public Health Disaster in the Making," *American*, June 3, 2009.

Callaghan, Peter. "Is Smoking Ban in Parks About Health or Power?" *News Tribune* (Tacoma, WA), March 3, 2009.

Christian Science Monitor, "Hollywood Kicks a Noxious Habit," August 1, 2007.

Cincotta, Joan. "Smoked Out: Campaign Seeks to End Smoking in Movies Rated for Kids," *Post-Standard* (Syracuse, NY), December 1, 2008.

Constatinides, Apollon. "Give Workers Tools to Kick Habit," *Atlanta Journal-Constitution*, November 25, 2009.

Dys, Andrew. "Smoking Ban Irks a Few, Pleases Many More," *Herald* (Rock Hill, SC), May 2, 2009.

Engel, Jeremy. "KY. Should Raise the Smoking Age to 21," *Kentucky Post* (Covington, KY), March 4, 2005.

Firey, Thomas A. "Smoking Bans Are Dangerous to a Free Society's Health," *Baltimore Sun*, December 6, 2006.

Firey, Thomas A., and Jacob Grier, "Please Do Smoke, if You Like," *Washington Post*, January 20, 2008.

Flynn, Ed. "Why Can't Government Give Up Tobacco?" *Albany Times Union*, August 2, 2009.

Gordon, Rachel. "San Francisco May Expand Smoking Ban," *San Francisco Chronicle*, December 16, 2009.

Granias, Andy. "Time Is Right for State Smoking Ban," *Indiana Daily Student* (Bloomington, IN), November 1, 2007.

Heinemann, Gloria. "No Good Can Come from Using Tobacco," *Buffalo News* (Buffalo, NY), December 4, 2009.

Huffman, Todd. "Protect Children from Tobacco Smoke," *Register-Guard* (Eugene, OR), June 28, 2007.

Institute of Medicine, "Report Brief: Secondhand Smoke Exposure and Cardiovascular Effects: Making Sense of the Evidence," October 2009.

Kane, Eugene. "Take It from an Ex-Smoker: Smoking Ban Is a Good Thing," *Milwaukee Journal Sentinel*, May 7, 2009.

Levy, Robert A. "Smoking Bans Continue an Assault on Freedom," *Arizona Republic*, October 24, 2005.

Martin, Roland. "Commentary: High Cigarette Tax? Great?" CNN, March 31, 2009.

McClellan, Bill. "Blowing Smoke on Secondhand Smoke," *St. Louis Post-Dispatch*, August 21, 2009.

McNeil, Stacy A. "Tobacco Control Works: Don't Cut It," *Post-Standard* (Syracuse, NY), November 23, 2009.

Mineau, Margaret E. "Tobacco Control Helps Save Lives," *Albany Times Union*, December 7, 2009.

Pion, Martin. "What Are We Waiting For? The Surgeon General Declared Secondhand Smoke Dangerous 23 Years Ago," *St. Louis Post-Dispatch*, June 2, 2009.

Radmacher, Dan. "Smoking Ban Will Make a Real Difference," *Roanoke Times*, March 1, 2009.

Robson, David. "Have the Tobacco Police Gone Too Far?" *New Scientist*, April 1, 2009.

Saletan, William. "Vapor War: Our Irrational Hostility Toward Electronic Cigarettes," *Slate*, June 3, 2009.

Saunders, Debra J. "Nanny State Becomes Granny State," *San Francisco Chronicle*, October 14, 2007.

Siegel, Michael. "Enough Secondhand Hysteria: Anti-Smoking Groups Exaggerate Risks to Justify Ban in City Parks," *NY Daily News*, October 26, 2009.

Skapinker, Michael. "Slipping Out for a Cigarette," *Financial Times*, September 29, 2009.

Snowdon, Christopher. "Beyond Belief," VelvetGloveIronFist.com, January 8, 2009.

Soliman, Ahmed. "Latest Anti-Smoking Measure Goes Too Far," *Record* (Bergen County, NJ), September 24, 2009.

State (Columbia, SC), "Improve S.C. in One Easy Step: Raise Cigarette Tax," January 17, 2010.

Strom, David. "None of Your Business!" Townhall.com, March 13, 2008.

Sullum, Jacob. "A Pack of Lies: The Surgeon General Hypes the Hazards of Secondhand Smoke," *Reason*, July 5, 2006.

Sun News (Myrtle Beach, SC), "Smoke-Free Surfside," October 2, 2007.

Washington Times, "Unlucky Strike: Military Smoking Ban Puts Troops in Danger," July 16, 2009.

Winickoff, Jonathan P., Joan Friebely, Susanne E. Tanski, Cheryl Sherrod, Georg E. Matt, Melbourne F. Hovell, and Robert C. McMillen. "Beliefs About the Health Effects of 'Thirdhand' Smoke and Home Smoking Bans," *Pediatrics*, January 2009.

Web Sites

Center for Public Accountability in Tobacco Control (www.tobacco controlintegrity.com). This Web site contains information and commentary on tobacco control policies in the United States.

The Tobacco Institute (www.tobaccoinstitute.com). This Web site provides the public with documents related to tobacco litigation regarding smoking and health.

Truth Campaign (www.thetruth.com). This Web site is part of a youth-focused antitobacco education campaign that contains information about the tobacco industry.

Index

A
Abstinence policy, 20–21, 23–24
Acetaldehyde, 14
Action on Smoking and Health (ASH), 76
Addiction
  methods of overcoming, 16–18
  to nicotine, 13–15, 90
  withdrawal symptoms from, 15
Adolescents
  antismoking programs aimed at, 90–92
  attitudes of, toward smoking, 44–45
  declining smoking rates among, 40–45
  risk for addiction in, 14–15
  See also Teen smoking
Air filtration, 73–74
Alcabes, Philip, 19–24
American Legacy Foundation, 92
American Stop Smoking Intervention Study (ASSIST), 98
Americans with Disabilities Act (ADA), 79
Ammonia, 15
Aneurysm, 15
Angieri, Yvonne, 71–75

Antismoking campaigns
  do not work, 94–99
  help reduce smoking, 89–93
Anti-smoking movement, 8–9, 63–64
Asman, K., 46–51
Asthma, 79

B
Bachman, Jerald, 41
Banzhaf, John, 76–82
Bars
  smoking should be banned in, 65–70
  smoking should not be banned in, 71–75
Basham, Patrick, 94–99
Behavioral treatments, for quitting smoking, 16
Bhutan, 63
Bloomberg, Michael R., 95
Brain, effect of tobacco on, 13–15
Breske, Roger, 68
Bronchitis, 15, 79
Bupropion, 17

C
Campaign for Tobacco-Free Kids Action Fund, 55, 56, 57, 97
Cancer, 13, 15, 23, 27
Carabollo, R., 46–51

Picture Credits

AP Images, 22, 28, 34, 56, 62, 74, 81, 108, 119
Cengage/Gale, 17, 21, 29, 42, 50, 57, 61, 68, 73, 96, 104, 113, 120
Chip East/Reuters/Landov, 85
Robert Giroux/MCT/Landov, 97
Image copyright © Gelpi, 2010. Used under license from Shutterstock.com, 14
Image copyright © Jozsef Szasz-Fabian, 2010. Used under license from Shutterstock.com, 88
Image copyright © Mark William Richardson, 2010. Used under license from Shutterstock.com, 52
Image copyright © Vasilchenko Nikita, 2010. Used under license from Shutterstock.com, 11
Kevin Lamarque/Reuters/Landov, 67
Milk & Honey Creative/Getty Images, 43
Eduardo Sverdlin/UPI/Landov, 115
Mario Tama/Getty Images, 102
Roger L. Wollenberg/UPI/Landov, 91
© WorldFoto/Alamy, 48